Stegosaurus

Sinosauropteryx

Tyrannosaurus

Szechuanosaurus

Tianyulong

Mamenchisaurus

Centrosaurus

Wuerhosaurus

Miragaia

Microraptor

Dromaeosaurus

Spinosaurus

Wuerhosaurus

Huayangosaurus

Saichania

Centrosaurus

Rajasaurus

Stygimoloch

Szechuanosaurus

Olorotitan

Triceratops

Therizinosaurus

Tianyulong

Microraptor

Mononykus

Nodosaurus

Sinosauropteryx

Tyrannosaurus

Miragaia

Protoceratops

Stegoceras

Tatisaurus

Stegoceras

Dromaeosaurus

Stygimoloch

Tatisaurus

Mononykus

PNSO Encyclopedia for Children

THE SECRETS OF DINOSAURS

PNSO Encyclopedia for Children
THE SECRETS OF DINOSAURS

Illustrations: ZHAO Chuang / Text: YANG Yang

A PNSO Production

BROWN BOOKS KIDS

PNSO Encyclopedia for Children: The Secrets of Dinosaurs by Yang Yang and Zhao Chuang

Brown Books Kids
16250 Knoll Trail Drive, Suite 205
Dallas / New York
www.BrownBooksKids.com
(972) 381-0009

A New Era in Publishing®

Publisher's Cataloging-In-Publication Data

Names: Yang, Yang (Writer of children's encyclopedia) author. | Zhao, Chuang, illustrator. | Hill, Degan, translator. | PNSO (Organization), production company.
Title: The secrets of dinosaurs / illustrations: ZHAO Chuang ; text: YANG Yang ; [translator, Degan Hill].
Description: Dallas ; New York : Brown Books Kids, [an imprint of] Brown Books Publishing Group, [2021] | Series: PNSO encyclopedia for children | Translated from the Chinese published in 2015. | "A PNSO production." | Interest age level: 010-012. | Include bibliographical references and index. | Summary: "Filled with incredible facts and history about the most famous reptiles to ever roam this earth, The Secrets of Dinosaurs is the perfect book for any child interested in dinosaurs"--Provided by publisher.
Identifiers: ISBN 9781612545158
Subjects: LCSH: Dinosaurs--Encyclopedias, Juvenile. | CYAC: Dinosaurs--Encyclopedias.
Classification: LCC QE861.5 .Y36 2021 | DDC 567.903--dc23

ISBN 978-1-61254-515-8
LCCN 2020921423

Printed in China
11 10 9 8 7 6 5 4 3

For more information or to contact the author, please go to www.BrownBooks.com.

This book is dedicated to:

Sir Isaac Newton, President of the Royal Society, England.
We thank him for his extraordinary contribution to science,
which has led us to a more civilized society.

A Sketch of *Tyrannosaurus*

Contents List

xii | Foreword

xiii | Author's Preface

2 | Notes for Reading

4 | The Incredible Dinosaurs

6 | Back to the World of Dinosaurs

8 | Main Content

212 | Index

214 | References

218 | About the Authors

Table of Contents

8 Origins of Saurischian Fossils

10 Period of Existence of Saurischian Fossils in the Mesozoic Era

Theropoda

12 | *Monolophosaurus*: Crested fast-moving hunter

14 | *Irritator*: The fossil scientists had some irritation with!

16 | The largest carnivorous dinosaur: *Spinosaurus*

18 | The first dinosaur to be named: *Megalosaurus*

20 | The hunter that relies on its hearing: *Herrerasaurus*

22 | A dinosaur with two crests: *Dilophosaurus*

24 | *Coelophysis*: Wow, it has been to space!

26 | Even its friends don't trust the *Majungasaurus*

28 | The speedy giant: *Abelisaurus*

30 | The brave and battle-tested *Rajasaurus*

32 | An accidental find: *Gasosaurus*

34 | Most ferocious Jurassic dinosaur: *Allosaurus*

36 | Spoiled for choices: *Szechuanosaurus*

38 | The most powerful dinosaur of the Jurassic period: *Yangchuanosaurus*

40 | The pocket-sized king of present-day Australia: *Australovenator*

42 | The giant head of the *Giganotosaurus*

44 | A crowned member of the tyrannosaur family: *Guanlong*

46 | Feathered ancestor of *Tyrannosaurus rex*: *Dilong*

48 | The world's most ferocious dinosaur: *Tyrannosaurus rex*

50 | *Compsognathus*: The dinosaur with a very beautiful jaw!

52 | The beautiful *Sinocalliopteryx* and its unforgiving jaws

54 | I've seen those colors before: *Sinosauropteryx*

56 | A feathered dinosaur: *Beipiaosaurus*

58 | It is like a big ostrich: *Archaeornithomimus*

60 | *Mononykus*: Its claw looks so lonely!

62 | One of the smallest dinosaurs: *Hesperonychus*

64 | The little fairy with four wings: *Microraptor*

66 | *Buitreraptors* hunting a *Gasparinisaura*

68 | The *Deinonychus* and its pair of scary-looking claws

70 | The perfect hunter: *Utahraptor*

Sauropodomorpha

72 | The crafty hunter: *Velociraptor*

74 | Flapping its wings like a bird: *Sinornithosaurus*

76 | The silent hunter: *Luanchuanraptor*

78 | The little dinosaur with short arms: *Tianyuraptor*

80 | A real team worker: *Dromaeosauroides*

82 | Working together to kill their enemies: *Dromaeosaurus*

84 | *Oviraptor* wasn't stealing eggs

86 | The magical feathers of the *Caudipteryx*

88 | Armed with both speed and power: The killer *Gigantoraptor*

90 | The *Epidendrosaurus*: What is it digging?

92 | *Epidexipteryx*: It can spread its tail feathers open just like a peacock!

94 | *Lufengosaurus*: Who's chasing me?

96 | *Plateosaurus*: The dinosaur with feline claws

98 | Doubtful largest dinosaur: *Amphicoelias*

100 | The longest animal on land: *Diplodocus*

102 | A little thing getting kicked around: *Europasaurus*

104 | The tallest dinosaur: *Sauroposeidon*

106 | A dinosaur with feet like discs: *Euhelopus*

108 | *Mamenchisaurus*: Part of its body is like a long bridge

110 | It is content with being an ordinary dinosaur: *Omeisaurus*

112 | *Shunosaurus*: Its tail has a secret weapon!

114 | Its body is covered with "grapes": *Ampelosaurus*

116 | *Dongyangosaurus*: Where is the best place to give birth to a baby?

118 | The big fellow walking around with feet turned out: *Daxiatitan*

120 | The chubbiest dinosaur of the dinosaur world: *Huanghetitan*

122 | *Argentinosaurus*: Used to be world's largest

Table of Contents

124 Origins of Ornithischian Fossils

126 Period of Existence of Ornithischian Fossils in the Mesozoic Era

Ornithopoda

128 | A champion runner: *Dryosaurus*

130 | One of the most famous dinosaurs: *Iguanodon*

132 | *Jintasaurus*: Its discovery suggests hadrosaurs might have originated in Asia

134 | Its thumbs are similar to large thorns: *Jinzhousaurus*

136 | The dinosaur with a "sail" on its back: *Ouranosaurus*

138 | Speaking with its big nose: *Altirhinus*

140 | A crest that grows with age: *Corythosaurus*

142 | Crested "duck": *Tsintaosaurus*

144 | A crest like a fan: *Olorotitan*

146 | The dinosaur that sings: *Parasaurolophus*

148 | The dinosaur fossil that was used to treat diseases: *Shantungosaurus*

150 | The dinosaur with the most teeth: *Hadrosaurus*

152 | China's first dinosaur: *Mandschurosaurus*

154 | A giant "duck": *Anatotitan*

156 | A responsible and caring parent: *Maiasaura*

158 | More than one thousand teeth: *Edmontosaurus*

Marginocephalia

160 | Always wearing a hat: *Stegoceras*

162 | A magical dinosaur: *Dracorex*

164 | The dinosaur with "bumps": *Pachycephalosaurus*

166 | A ceratopsian without a horn: *Yinlong*

168 | The North American *Leptoceratops*: What a cute dinosaur

170 | Don't break my eggs!: *Archaeoceratops*

172 | With a mouth like that of a cute little parrot: *Psittacosaurus*

174 | With many beautiful and formidable horns: *Sinoceratops*

176 | The dinosaur with the most horns: *Styracosaurus*

178 | The single-horned warrior: *Centrosaurus*

180 | *Torosaurus*: Its head is equal to thirteen human heads in size

182 | The most famous member of the *Ceratopsidae* family: *Triceratops*

Thyreophora

184 | Without any bone plates or spikes: *Tatisaurus*

186 | The dinosaur with the most bone plates on its back: *Huayangosaurus*

188 | Strange bony plates: *Kentrosaurus*

190 | The long-necked *Miragaia*

192 | "General" *Gigantspinosaurus*: It carries a sword on its shoulders

194 | Its shoulder spikes stick straight up: *Tuojiangosaurus*

196 | Its back is covered with rectangular "toy bricks": *Wuerhosaurus*

198 | Most famous stegosaurian: *Stegosaurus*

200 | Like an enormous hedgehog: *Polacanthus*

202 | *Sauropelta*: It has a really long tail!

204 | Australia's armored fighter: *Kunbarrasaurus*

206 | Perfect armor: *Saichania*

208 | Enjoying breakfast: *Zhongyuansaurus*

210 | The armored warrior: *Ankylosaurus*

Foreword

Paleontologist Curator and Chairman of the Division of Paleontology, AMNH Science Consultant for English Publications of PNSO Dr. Mark A. Norell's Introduction to the Works by ZHAO Chuang and YANG Yang

I am a paleontologist at one of the world's great museums. I get to spend my days surrounded by dinosaur bones. Whether it is in Mongolia excavating, in China studying, in New York analyzing data, or anywhere on the planet writing, teaching, or lecturing, dinosaurs are not only my interest, but my livelihood.

Most scientists, even the most brilliant ones, work in very closed societies. A system which, no matter how hard they try, is still unapproachable to average people. Maybe it's due to the complexities of mathematics, difficulties in understanding molecular biochemistry, or reconciling complex theory with actual data. No matter what, this behavior fosters boredom and disengagement. Personality comes in as well, and most scientists lack the communication skills necessary to make their efforts interesting and approachable. People are left intimidated by science. But dinosaurs are special—people of all ages love them. So dinosaurs foster a great opportunity to teach science to everyone by tapping into something everyone is interested in.

That's why Yang Yang and Zhao Chuang are so important. Both are extraordinarily talented and very smart, but neither are scientists. Instead they use art and words as a medium to introduce dinosaur science to everyone from small children to grandparents—and even to scientists working in other fields!

Zhao Chuang's paintings, sculptures, drawings, and films are state-of-the-art representations of how these fantastic animals looked and behaved. They are drawn from the latest discoveries and his close collaboration with leading paleontologists. Yang Yang's writing is more than mere description. Instead she weaves stories through the narrative or makes the descriptions engaging and humorous. The subjects are so approachable that her stories can be read to small children, and young readers can discover these animals and explore science on their own. Through our fascination with dinosaurs, important concepts of geology, biology, and evolution are learned in a fun way. Zhao Chuang and Yang Yang are the world's best, and it is an honor to work with them.

Mark Norell

Author's Preface

We are not alone in this world; we share it with others.
—A word to the fathers and mothers of our young readers

As I write this, I am sitting in the shade of my courtyard. Above in the trees, the cicadas are incessantly chirping, with their noises filling the air. Since the beginning of late spring, they have been happily chirping away every day. Happily? Well, I rarely see them; they are either hiding deep down in the dark soil biding their time until they reach maturity, or lying on the tree branches, enjoying a reclusive life. I know this without having to see them. As I listen to the sounds which tease my ear, I know that they are living a merry life in the world that we share with them.

At this moment, my daughter is chasing an ant that is moving on the ground; occasionally, she interrupts me with her giggles. She finds leaves which were blown off the trees by wind the night before and are now lying on the ground. Picking them up in bunches, she comes over to show me her new discovery. I tell her that these are leaves that have fallen from the trees. Soon after, she grabs a few rose petals, acting as if she is going to consume them. I quickly instruct her that these are flowers and that flowers cannot be eaten. Maybe she does not understand what I am saying; she has just learned to crawl, and she is still unable to talk. Because of this she probably does not recognize

and identify the ants, leaves, and flowers, but nevertheless, she gets great enjoyment from watching them, just as she does from seeing me, as she giggles playfully. For her, there are very few differences between the ants, leaves, and flowers on the one hand, and her mom and dad, aunts and uncles on the other. She has great curiosity toward all these things which share this world with her.

I can't really identify at what point adults gradually begin to lose this magical sense of curiosity, or when we begin to overlook all of the other types of life and arrogantly consider humans as the most important subjects, simply because now we are the predominant group on this planet.

The irony is that if there is no other life, humans would no longer be able to support themselves and would perish. However, we often do not think in this way. We are accustomed to understanding life through such a paradigm: chicken is delicious food, from which you can make roast chicken or smoked chicken; the beef we get from cattle tastes good and has high nutritional value. We are often indoctrinated with such knowledge, so it is no surprise that this often inadvertently breeds our selfish arrogance.

I often find myself thinking about this problem, so for the longest time, I have desired to write an encyclopedia for children, one that introduces them to a wide variety of other types of life. This encyclopedic book should not be like ones written for adults; it is not merely a large number of details showing an animal's length, height, and weight. Its purpose is to be far more than a pile of data, to go beyond just a list of knowledge and facts; the essence of this work is meant to be like the chorus of afternoon cicadas. You cannot see them, yet you hear their voices, just like those ants which my daughter finds enchanting—you forge a close connection with them despite not knowing their specifics. For children, everything in this world is incredibly fresh. They want to know: beyond themselves, their family, their kindergarten teachers, and fellow students, what else is out there in this world? In addition to their home, their kindergarten, and the city that they live in, how much further beyond does this world extend to? They want to move beyond the present and the past that they can remember to know how far the world will go. Their curiosity is a key which unlocks the entire world. All they ask us is to leave the door open. They can figure out the rest on their own.

Hence, our collection of stories within the PNSO Encyclopedia for Children is meant to impress our children with an understanding of the world beyond humans. Children should realize that this world is not only for us; others share it with us. The "others" may be other forms of life or something wonderful that exists in our human imagination. In short, these exist in our present world, whether in our day-to-day reality or the magical expanses of our imagination.

To be aware of their existence is more than a form of knowledge. It is a strength by which our inner world expands and broadens. If that happens, we will be less likely to become arrogant because of our ignorance, to begrudge small things, or to hinder our long-term future because of immediate gains. We can avoid being selfish, narrow-minded, and fearful. We should respect all lives because they have accompanied us throughout our existence and are sharing this world with us. The world is so dauntingly big; it is vital that we work together in harmony with each other to move forward.

Often, the babbling of a young child reminds me how important it is to keep alive the curiosity of childhood. It is that curiosity that allows us to walk humbly in this vast world. I hope that as you read this book with your children, you may nurture their sense of curiosity and accompany them in exploring this wondrous world.

杨杨
YANG Yang
August 1, 2015, in Beijing

A sketch of *Velociraptor*

Notes for Reading

1 **Period of Existence of Dinosaurs**
(for selected species)

2 **Scales:** 50 cm, 1 m, 5 m, 25 m
Reference objects: basketball, father, mother, boy, girl, bus, airplane
Diagrams showing dinosaurs' sizes: dinosaur's silhouette (when the size of the dinosaur is less than 1 unit of the scale), dinosaur's outline

Millions of Years Ago	252.17 ±0.06	~247.2		~237			201.3 ±0.2		174.1 ±1.0	163 ±1
Epoch	Early Triassic	Middle Triassic			Late Triassic			Early Jurassic		Middle Jurassic
Period				Triassic					Jurassic	
Era										
Eon										

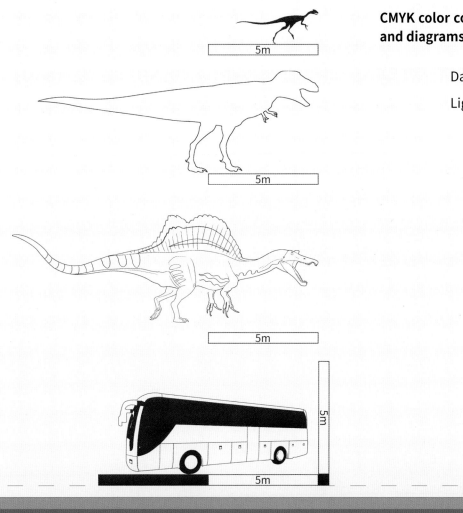

CMYK color codes for scales, reference objects, and diagrams showing dinosaurs' sizes

Dark background: C0 M0 Y0 K80

Light background: C0 M0 Y0 K20

5m

5m

5m

5m

25m

~145.0   100.5   66.0

Late Jurassic   Early Cretaceous   Late Cretaceous

Cretaceous

Mesozoic

Phanerozoic Eon

The Incredible Dinosaurs

Two hundred thirty-five million years ago, magical reptiles existed on Earth. We now call them dinosaurs. It is hard to explain how far back 235 million years ago is. Anyway, that was a very long time ago, long before humans existed.

Dinosaurs were the dominant animals residing on Earth back then, just like we humans are today. The dinosaurs co-existed with many other creatures, so they were not lonely.

Many of the dinosaurs had enormous sizes, some were as large as three buses joined front to end, some as tall as a two-story building. We can only imagine how incredibly big they were. To keep their massive bodies functioning well, they had to eat all day long, and their appetites were as large as their body size. Some could swallow an entire mammal whole (which, in a way, is like them gobbling up our ancestors)! Nevertheless, there were also tiny dinosaurs that were smaller, like cute little kittens or chickens. Unfortunately, we could not keep them as pets, for although they were small in size, they were skilled fighters, like the bigger dinosaurs! The dinosaurs were the conquerors of the world hundreds of millions of years ago.

There are many types of dinosaurs, and they all looked different and lived in different ways. Some had horns on top of their heads, some had spikes on their backs; some consumed meat for survival whereas some only ate plants; some ran very fast, and some could fly in the sky . . . some of them were more fantastic than your wildest dreams!

The three geological periods when dinosaurs existed

Triassic Period 252–201 Million Years Ago
Jurassic Period 201–145 Million Years Ago
Cretaceous Period 145–66 Million Years Ago

Back to the World of Dinosaurs

It must be great to travel all over the world looking at the various types of dinosaurs! Sadly, it isn't possible anymore; the bad news is that they (by which I mean non-avian dinosaurs; mainstream scientists believe that birds are the modern-day descendants of dinosaurs) became extinct sixty-six million years ago, and they disappeared from the world forever, leaving nothing behind except for their fossils. It is a little depressing, but we can no longer go back to the age of dinosaurs!

Well, is it impossible for us to see dinosaurs anymore? Not exactly. I heard that this book can take us back in time and provide us with a glimpse into the age of dinosaurs.

Back to the age of dinosaurs? That's right!

Now let's take a ride in the time machine we have created with this book and travel back in time to visit the dinosaurs!

Fossils

Fossils are the preserved remains or traces of creatures from the remote past. There are many types of fossils; common dinosaur fossils include bones, skins, and footprints. By studying fossils, we can understand the paleoenvironment that they lived in and how they evolved over time.

Origins of Saurischian Fossils

Compiled by: PNSO

12 | *Monolophosaurus*
Fossil Origin: China, Asia

30 | *Rajasaurus*
Fossil Origin: India, Asia

33 | *Gasosaurus*
Fossil Origin: China, Asia

36 | *Szechuanosaurus*
Fossil Origin: China, Asia

38 | *Yangchuanosaurus*
Fossil Origin: China, Asia

44 | *Guanlong*
Fossil Origin: China, Asia

46 | *Dilong*
Fossil Origin: China, Asia

53 | *Sinocalliopteryx*
Fossil Origin: China, Asia

54 | *Sinosauropteryx*
Fossil Origin: China, Asia

56 | *Beipiaosaurus*
Fossil Origin: China, Asia

59 | *Archaeornithomimus*
Fossil Origin: China, Uzbekistan, Asia

60 | *Mononykus*
Fossil Origin: Mongolia, Asia

65 | *Microraptor*
Fossil Origin: China, Asia

73 | *Velociraptor*
Fossil Origin: Mongolia, China, Asia

74 | *Sinornithosaurus*
Fossil Origin: China, Asia

76 | *Luanchuanraptor*
Fossil Origin: China, Asia

78 | *Tianyuraptor*
Fossil Origin: China, Asia

84 | *Oviraptor*
Fossil Origin: Asia, Mongolia, China

86 | *Caudipteryx*
Fossil Origin: China, Asia

89 | *Gigantoraptor*
Fossil Origin: China, Asia

91 | *Epidendrosaurus*
Fossil Origin: China, Asia

92 | *Epidexipteryx*
Fossil Origin: China, Asia

95 | *Lufengosaurus*
Fossil Origin: China, Asia

107 | *Euhelopus*
Fossil Origin: China, Asia

108 | *Mamenchisaurus*
Fossil Origin: China, Asia

110 | *Omeisaurus*
Fossil Origin: China, Asia

112 | *Shunosaurus*
Fossil Origin: China, Asia

116 | *Dongyangosaurus*
Fossil Origin: China, Asia

119 | *Daxiatitan*
Fossil Origin: China, Asia

120 | *Huanghetitan*
Fossil Origin: China, Asia

41 | *Australovenator*
Fossil Origin: Australia, Oceania

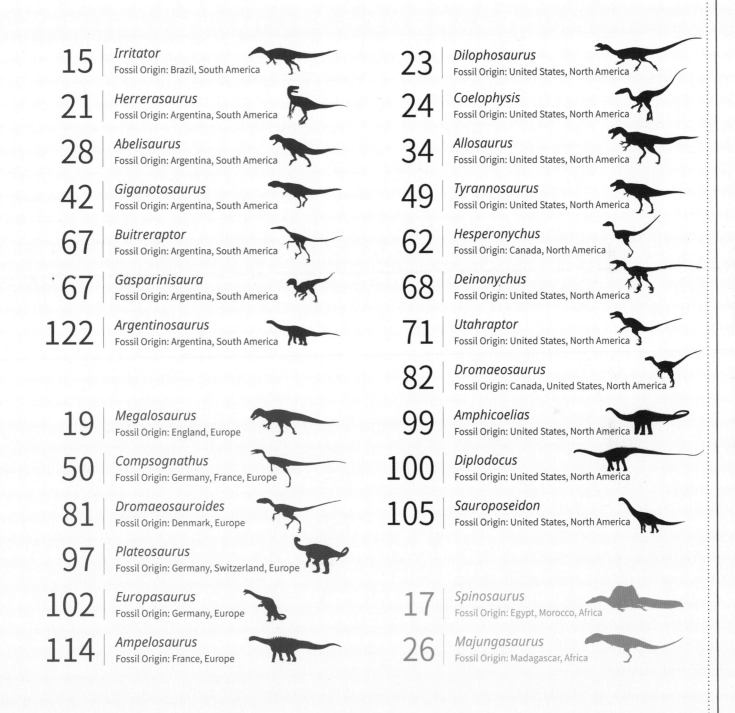

15 | *Irritator*
Fossil Origin: Brazil, South America

21 | *Herrerasaurus*
Fossil Origin: Argentina, South America

28 | *Abelisaurus*
Fossil Origin: Argentina, South America

42 | *Giganotosaurus*
Fossil Origin: Argentina, South America

67 | *Buitreraptor*
Fossil Origin: Argentina, South America

67 | *Gasparinisaura*
Fossil Origin: Argentina, South America

122 | *Argentinosaurus*
Fossil Origin: Argentina, South America

19 | *Megalosaurus*
Fossil Origin: England, Europe

50 | *Compsognathus*
Fossil Origin: Germany, France, Europe

81 | *Dromaeosauroides*
Fossil Origin: Denmark, Europe

97 | *Plateosaurus*
Fossil Origin: Germany, Switzerland, Europe

102 | *Europasaurus*
Fossil Origin: Germany, Europe

114 | *Ampelosaurus*
Fossil Origin: France, Europe

23 | *Dilophosaurus*
Fossil Origin: United States, North America

24 | *Coelophysis*
Fossil Origin: United States, North America

34 | *Allosaurus*
Fossil Origin: United States, North America

49 | *Tyrannosaurus*
Fossil Origin: United States, North America

62 | *Hesperonychus*
Fossil Origin: Canada, North America

68 | *Deinonychus*
Fossil Origin: United States, North America

71 | *Utahraptor*
Fossil Origin: United States, North America

82 | *Dromaeosaurus*
Fossil Origin: Canada, United States, North America

99 | *Amphicoelias*
Fossil Origin: United States, North America

100 | *Diplodocus*
Fossil Origin: United States, North America

105 | *Sauroposeidon*
Fossil Origin: United States, North America

17 | *Spinosaurus*
Fossil Origin: Egypt, Morocco, Africa

26 | *Majungasaurus*
Fossil Origin: Madagascar, Africa

 Asia   **South America**   **Africa**   **Europe**   **North America**   **Oceania**

Period of Existence of Saurischian Fossils in the Mesozoic Era

Compiled by: PNSO

21 | *Herrerasaurus*
Triassic Period

24 | *Coelophysis*
Triassic Period

97 | *Plateosaurus*
Triassic Period

12 | *Monolophosaurus*
Jurassic Period

19 | *Megalosaurus*
Jurassic Period

23 | *Dilophosaurus*
Jurassic Period

33 | *Gasosaurus*
Jurassic Period

34 | *Allosaurus*
Jurassic Period

36 | *Szechuanosaurus*
Jurassic Period

38 | *Yangchuanosaurus*
Jurassic Period

44 | *Guanlong*
Jurassic Period

50 | *Compsognathus*
Jurassic Period

91 | *Epidendrosaurus*
Jurassic Period

92 | *Epidexipteryx*
Jurassic Period

95 | *Lufengosaurus*
Jurassic Period

99 | *Amphicoelias*
Jurassic Period

100 | *Diplodocus*
Jurassic Period

102 | *Europasaurus*
Jurassic Period

108 | *Mamenchisaurus*
Jurassic Period

110 | *Omeisaurus*
Jurassic Period

112 | *Shunosaurus*
Jurassic Period

15 | *Irritator*
Cretaceous Period

17 | *Spinosaurus*
Cretaceous Period

26 | *Majungasaurus*
Cretaceous Period

28 | *Abelisaurus*
Cretaceous Period

30 | *Rajasaurus*
Cretaceous Period

Millions of Years Ago	252.17 ±0.06	~247.2	~237		201.3 ±0.2		174.1 ±1.0	163. ±1.
Epoch	Early Triassic	Middle Triassic	Late Triassic		Early Jurassic		Middle Jurassic	
Period		Triassic				Jurassic		
Era								
Eon								

41	Australovenator Cretaceous Period
42	Giganotosaurus Cretaceous Period
46	Dilong Cretaceous Period
49	Tyrannosaurus Cretaceous Period	76	Luanchuanraptor Cretaceous Period
53	Sinocalliopteryx Cretaceous Period	78	Tianyuraptor Cretaceous Period
54	Sinosauropteryx Cretaceous Period	81	Dromaeosauroides Cretaceous Period
56	Beipiaosaurus Cretaceous Period	82	Dromaeosaurus Cretaceous Period
59	Archaeornithomimus Cretaceous Period	84	Oviraptor Cretaceous Period
60	Mononykus Cretaceous Period	86	Caudipteryx Cretaceous Period
62	Hesperonychus Cretaceous Period	89	Gigantoraptor Cretaceous Period
65	Microraptor Cretaceous Period	105	Sauroposeidon Cretaceous Period
67	Buitreraptor Cretaceous Period	107	Euhelopus Cretaceous Period
67	Gasparinisaura Cretaceous Period	114	Ampelosaurus Cretaceous Period
68	Deinonychus Cretaceous Period	116	Dongyangosaurus Cretaceous Period
71	Utahraptor Cretaceous Period	119	Daxiatitan Cretaceous Period
73	Velociraptor Cretaceous Period	120	Huanghetitan Cretaceous Period
74	Sinornithosaurus Cretaceous Period	122	Argentinosaurus Cretaceous Period

~145.0   100.5   66.0

Late Jurassic   Early Cretaceous   Late Cretaceous

Cretaceous

Mesozoic

Phanerozoic Eon

Monolophosaurus
Crested fast-moving hunter

Many dinosaurs, such as *Monolophosaurus*, *Dilophosaurus*, and *Guanlong*, had distinct crests. *Monolophosaurus* and *Dilophosaurus* had similar names, suggesting that their crests were similar, with the difference being that the latter had one more. In fact, their crests had similar functions such as for display and attracting the opposite sex. The five-meter-long *Monolophosaurus* was an agile predator.

Millions of Years Ago	252.17 ±0.06	~247.2	~237		201.3 ±0.2		174.1 ±1.0	163.5 ±1.0
Epoch	Early Triassic	Middle Triassic	Late Triassic			Early Jurassic	Middle Jurassic	
Period			Triassic				Jurassic	
Era								
Eon								

Monolophosaurus

Body size: 5 meters in length

Diet: Carnivorous

Period of existence: Jurassic

Fossil origin: China, Asia

5m

5m

~145.0

100.5

66.0

Late Jurassic

Early Cretaceous

Late Cretaceous

Cretaceous

Mesozoic

Phanerozoic Eon

Irritator
The fossil scientists had some irritation with!

To make the *Irritator*'s fossil complete, amateur paleontologists added many layers of plaster to its skull. Scientists painstakingly took a long time removing the plaster to reveal its exact shape. When they finally completed their work and thought about the irritation they had, they named this dinosaur *Irritator*.

The *Irritator* is a close relative of the largest carnivorous dinosaur, the *Spinosaurus*. Its head is decorated with a very peculiar-looking crown, and it enjoys eating fish.

Irritator

Body size: Approximately 8 meters in length
Diet: Fish
Period of existence: Cretaceous
Fossil origin: Brazil, South America

5m

5m

The fisherman
Spinosaurus

The *Spinosaurus* is one of the world's largest carnivorous dinosaurs. It is a very strange-looking dinosaur, with a head like that of a crocodile and a long, tall "fan" on its back. Because of its enormous size, it can quickly deal with its enemies and is able to hunt a variety of different types of prey. However, for some reason, this big fellow enjoys eating fish! It must look curious when it is hunting for fish!

Spinosaurus

Body size: 15 meters in length
Diet: Piscivorous
Period of existence: Cretaceous
Fossil origin: Morocco, Egypt, Africa

5m

5m

The first
dinosaur to be named
Megalosaurus

A dog's world is quite simple; it probably doesn't even know what the human word "dog" means. Likewise, the names of dinosaurs are also given by human beings. The *Megalosaurus* was the first dinosaur to be named by scientists. It was a ferocious carnivorous dinosaur, with a mouth full of sharp teeth.

Megalosaurus

Body size: 7–9 meters in length

Diet: Carnivorous

Period of existence: Jurassic

Fossil origin: United Kingdom, Europe

 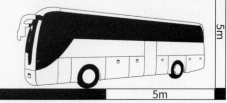

5m

5m

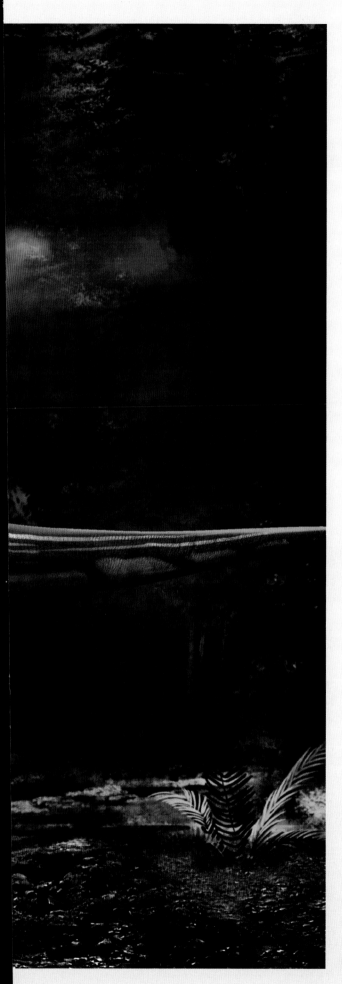

The hunter that relies on its hearing
Herrerasaurus

Can your ears hear sounds from very far away? The *Herrerasaurus*'s ears can because they are sensitive. It does not need to use its eyes to hunt for prey, but it relies on its specialized ears to catch prey instead. If a victim makes the slightest sound in the bushes, it will bolt towards the sound of its target and strike in a matter of seconds. Its slender body can act with great strength!

Herrerasaurus

Body size: 3–6 meters in length
Diet: Carnivorous
Period of existence: Triassic
Fossil origin: Argentina, South America

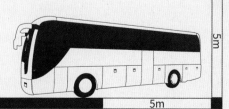

5m

5m

A dinosaur with two crests
Dilophosaurus

Have you ever seen an animal with a crest? There are roosters and crested cockatoos, but are there any others? Don't worry, if you can't think of more examples that exist in the modern-day world, you can find many others in the dinosaur world!

This *Dilophosaurus* has a crest, or crown, on its head. Its crown is shaped like a V—the sign for victory. In fact, the *Dilophosaurus* is so powerful and brave that it often wins battles, hence the sign fits this carnivorous dinosaur very well!

Dilophosaurus

Body size: 6 meters in length
Diet: Carnivorous
Period of existence: Jurassic
Fossil origin: United States, North America

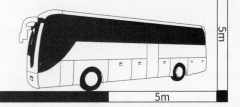

5m

5m

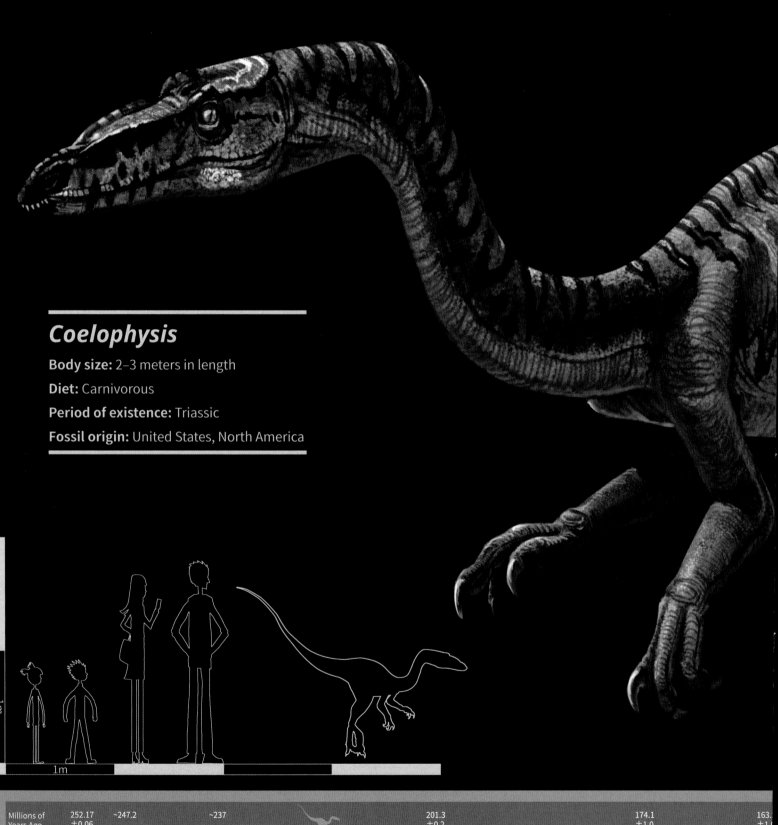

Coelophysis

Body size: 2–3 meters in length

Diet: Carnivorous

Period of existence: Triassic

Fossil origin: United States, North America

1m

1m

Millions of Years Ago	252.17 ±0.06	~247.2	~237		201.3 ±0.2	174.1 ±1.0	163. ±1.
Epoch	Early Triassic	Middle Triassic	Late Triassic			Early Jurassic	Middle Jurassic
Period	Triassic					Jurassic	
Era							
Eon							

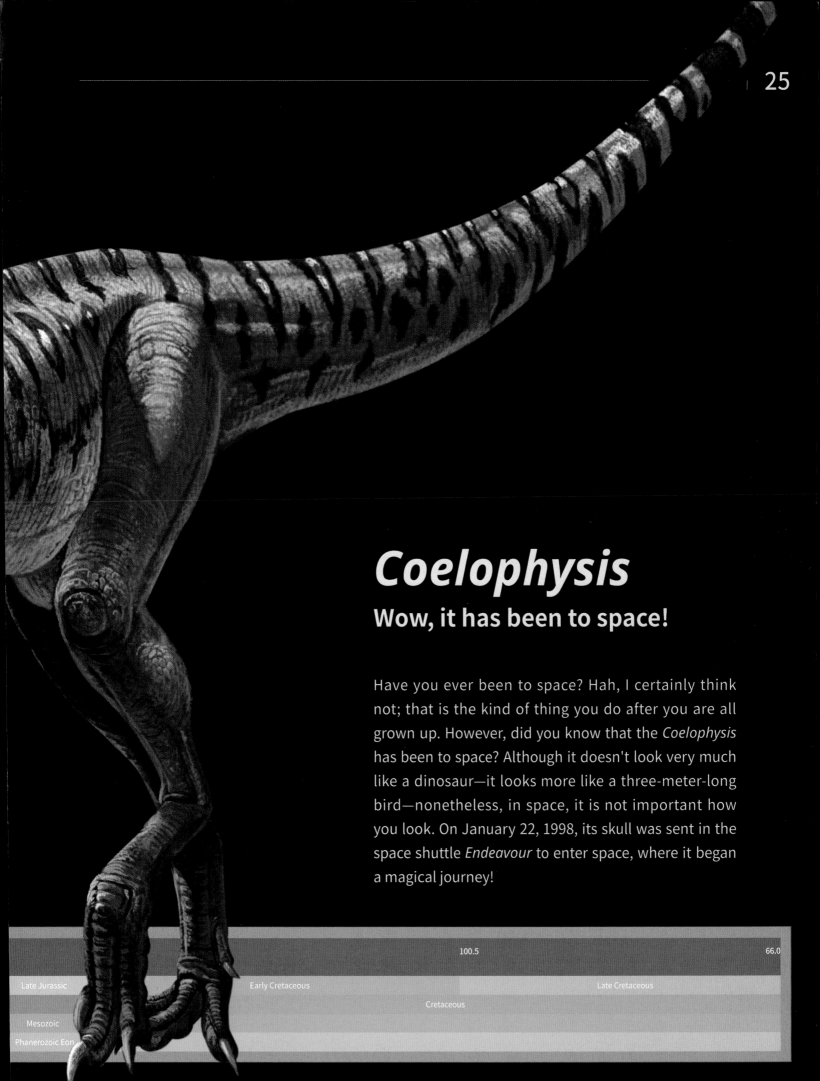

Coelophysis
Wow, it has been to space!

Have you ever been to space? Hah, I certainly think not; that is the kind of thing you do after you are all grown up. However, did you know that the *Coelophysis* has been to space? Although it doesn't look very much like a dinosaur—it looks more like a three-meter-long bird—nonetheless, in space, it is not important how you look. On January 22, 1998, its skull was sent in the space shuttle *Endeavour* to enter space, where it began a magical journey!

100.5

66.0

Late Jurassic

Early Cretaceous

Late Cretaceous

Cretaceous

Mesozoic

Phanerozoic Eon

Even its friends don't trust the
Majungasaurus

The *Majungasaurus* is only six to seven meters in length and weighs about 1.2 tons, which only counts as a medium-sized carnivorous dinosaur. However, it is well known for being very cruel. Scientists found that when it was starving, it would even eat its own friends. How awful!

Majungasaurus

Body size: 6–7 meters in length

Diet: Carnivorous

Period of existence: Cretaceous

Fossil origin: Madagascar, Africa

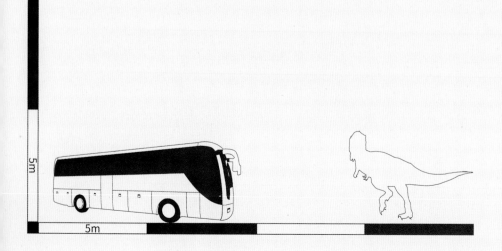

5m

5m

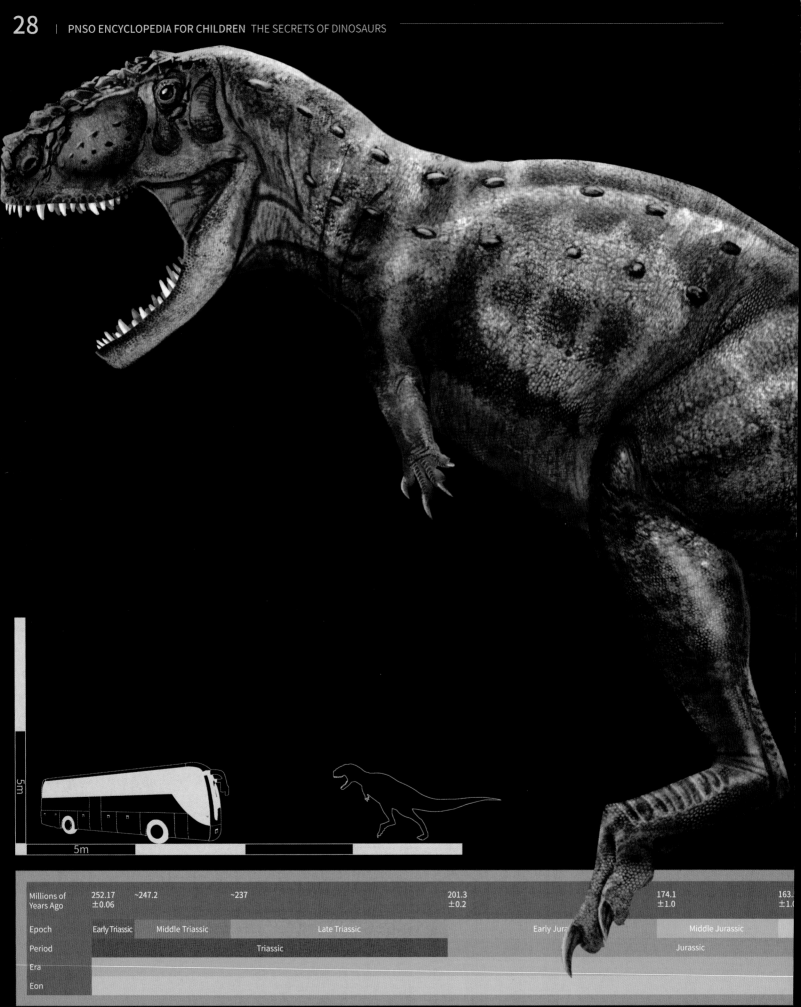

5m

5m

Millions of Years Ago	252.17 ±0.06	~247.2	~237		201.3 ±0.2			174.1 ±1.0	163. ±1.0
Epoch	Early Triassic	Middle Triassic	Late Triassic			Early Jura			Middle Jurassic
Period			Triassic					Jurassic	
Era									
Eon									

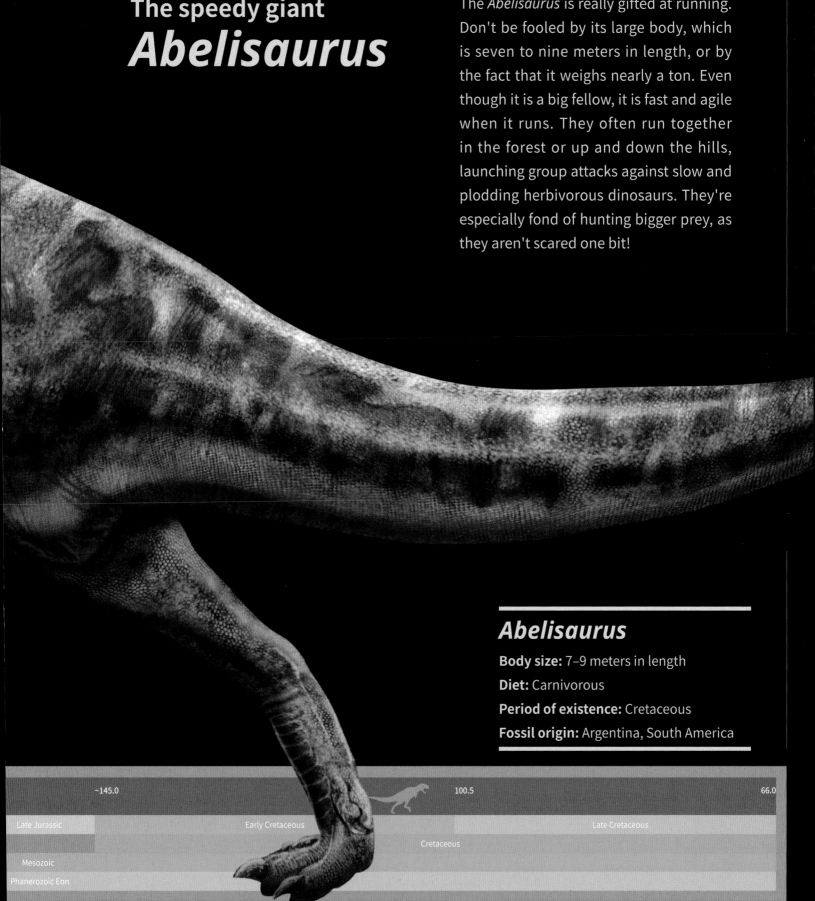

The speedy giant
Abelisaurus

The *Abelisaurus* is really gifted at running. Don't be fooled by its large body, which is seven to nine meters in length, or by the fact that it weighs nearly a ton. Even though it is a big fellow, it is fast and agile when it runs. They often run together in the forest or up and down the hills, launching group attacks against slow and plodding herbivorous dinosaurs. They're especially fond of hunting bigger prey, as they aren't scared one bit!

Abelisaurus

Body size: 7–9 meters in length
Diet: Carnivorous
Period of existence: Cretaceous
Fossil origin: Argentina, South America

~145.0	100.5	66.0
Late Jurassic	Early Cretaceous	Late Cretaceous
	Cretaceous	
Mesozoic		
Phanerozoic Eon		

The brave and battle-tested
Rajasaurus

Something good can be smelt in the air. An eight-meter-long *Rajasaurus* takes a deep breath and smells that! The *Rajasaurus* looks all around for the source and realizes that it is coming from a group of *Isisaurus*, which is its favorite food. The *Rajasaurus* cannot help himself from drooling greedily. Time to pick a snack!

Rajasaurus

Body size: 7–9 meters in length

Diet: Carnivorous

Period of existence: Cretaceous

Fossil origin: India, Asia

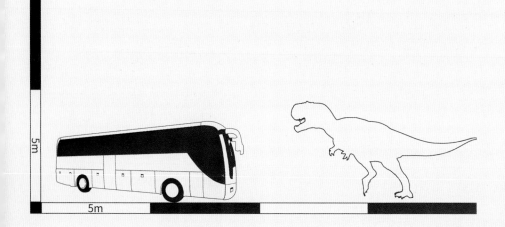

5m

5m

An accidental find
Gasosaurus

The first person to discover the *Gasosaurus* was not a scientist, but an explorer of the PetroChina Southwest Oil & Gasfield Company. The company was searching for natural gas, but in the end, discovered a *Gasosaurus* instead. The *Gasosaurus* was a fleet-footed dinosaur with a pair of keen eyes, which made it very easy to find its prey, even in the deepest, darkest parts of the woods.

Gasosaurus

Body size: Approximately 3.5 meters in length
Diet: Carnivorous
Period of existence: Jurassic
Fossil origin: China, Asia

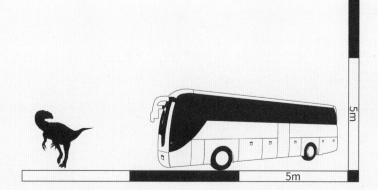

5m

5m

Most ferocious Jurassic dinosaur
Allosaurus

Do you know which was the greatest predator of the Jurassic? It was the *Allosaurus*. *Allosaurus* was not the largest carnivorous dinosaur. For example, *Torvosaurus*, which lived around them, was eleven meters long or bigger. But *Allosaurus* were excellent in many ways. They had sharp teeth that made their prey shudder, twenty-five-centimeter-long terrifying claws, and strong and fast-running legs. More importantly, they had an exceptionally clever brain, which made them the top local predators.

Allosaurus

Body size: 8–11 meters in length

Diet: Carnivorous

Period of existence: Jurassic

Fossil origin: United States, North America

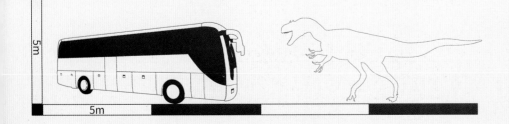

5m

5m

Spoiled for choices
Szechuanosaurus

Look, that eight-meter-long *Szechuanosaurus* over there looks furious. It's glaring angrily at that group of *Chuanjiesaurus* crossing a nearby path! Whats could be wrong? Oh, I get it, I think I can hear its stomach growling. It must be hungry as its mouth is dripping with drool! But why hasn't it attacked yet? The *Chuanjiesaurus* is its favorite food. Well, the *Szechuanosaurus* still hasn't picked one to attack because it can't decide which one is more delicious!

Goodness, what a greedy fellow!

Szechuanosaurus

Body size: Approximately 8 meters in length

Diet: Carnivorous

Period of existence: Jurassic

Fossil origin: China, Asia

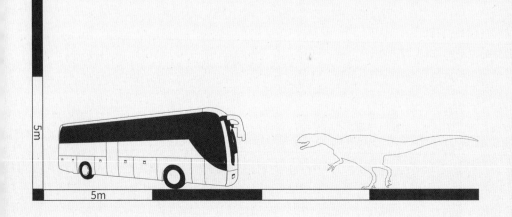

The most powerful dinosaur of the Jurassic period
Yangchuanosaurus

If you were to meet the *Yangchuanosaurus* during the age of the dinosaurs, you would turn around and run away as fast as possible. That's because it would open its terrifying mouth wide and chase after you. The *Yangchuanosaurus* was one of the most fearsome dinosaurs in present-day China during the Jurassic period, with its sharp teeth, terrifying claws, and a thick and powerful tail. It was an unforgiving predator and would challenge all prey.

5m

5m

Millions of Years Ago	252.17 ±0.06	~247.2	~237		201.3 ±0.?		174.1 ±1.0	163 ±1.
Epoch	Early Triassic	Middle Triassic	Late Triassic			rassic	Middle Jurassic	
Period			Triassic				Jurassic	
Era								
Eon								

Yangchuanosaurus

Body size: 7–9 meters in length

Diet: Carnivorous

Period of existence: Jurassic

Fossil origin: China, Asia

~145.0   100.5   66.0

Late   Early Cretaceous   Late Cretaceous

Cretaceous

Mesoz

Phanerozoic Eon

The pocket-sized king of present-day Australia
Australovenator

The *Australovenator* was tiny, and it didn't look very fierce; it looked rather cute! However, it was still a ferocious ruler over present-day Australia during the Cretaceous period. Its weapons were the curved claws on its forelimbs, which acted like a pair of guards.

Right now, a huge *Diamantinasaurus* is getting attacked by an *Australovenator*. Although the former is enormous, it is clumsy in the water and finds it hard to fight back. The *Australovenator* seizes the opportunity to bite at its neck viciously. Now it is time to use its scary-looking claws. They tear into the skin of its prey. Blood pours out from the open wounds, turning the water crimson red.

Australovenator

Body size: 6 meters in length
Diet: Carnivorous
Period of existence: Cretaceous
Fossil origin: Australia, Oceania

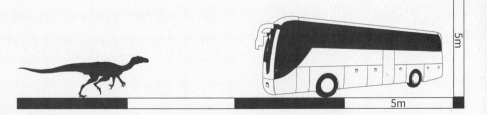

5m

5m

The giant head of the
Giganotosaurus

The *Giganotosaurus* is one of the most ferocious members of the dinosaur world, with the most noticeable characteristic being its enormous head. Its head is 1.6 meters long, which is more than your height. In addition to its giant head, it has many other big things; it has a huge body, and its sharp teeth and vicious-looking claws are also imposing. It uses all of these weapons to dominate the jungle.

5m

5m

Millions of Years Ago	252.17 ±0.06	~247.2	~237		201.3 ±0.2			174.1 ±1.0		163. ±1.
Epoch	Early Triassic	Middle Triassic		Late Triassic			Earl		le Jurassic	
Period			Triassic					Ju		
Era										
Eon										

Giganotosaurus

Body size: 12 meters in length

Diet: Carnivorous

Period of existence: Cretaceous

Fossil origin: Argentina, South America

100.5

66.0

Late Jurassic

Early Cretaceous

Late Cretaceous

Cretaceous

Mesozoic

Phanerozoic Eon

A crowned member of the tyrannosaur family
Guanlong

Although the *Guanlong* is rather small in size, it is one of the ancestors of the *Tyrannosaurus rex*. The *Guanlong* has a unique appearance; it has a brightly colored crown on its head, its body is covered with a layer of fur, and its forelimbs are covered in feathers, which look like wings. Although the *Guanlong* seems primitive, you can tell from its strong hind limbs, sharp teeth, and keen vision that it is still a fully fledged member of the tyrannosaur family, as there are many similarities between the *Tyrannosaurus rex* and the *Guanlong*.

Guanlong

Body size: 4–5 meters in length

Diet: Carnivorous

Period of existence: Jurassic

Fossil origin: China, Asia

5m

5m

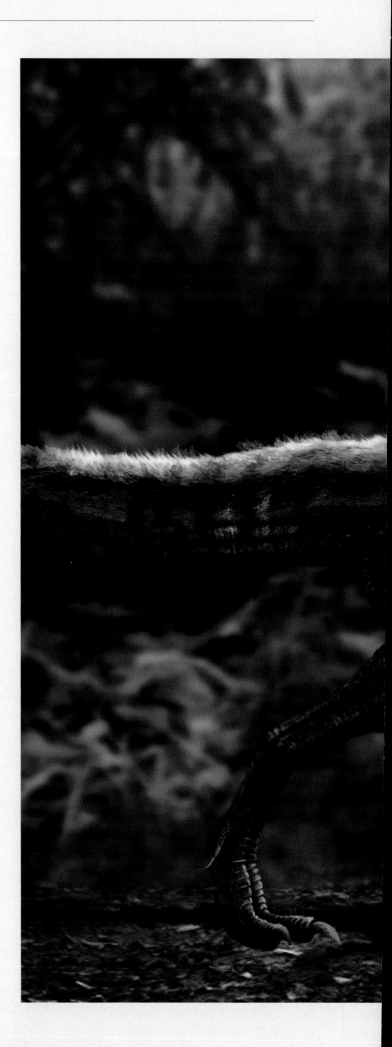

Dilong

Body size: Approximately 2 meters in length

Diet: Carnivorous

Period of existence: Cretaceous

Fossil origin: China, Asia

Feathered ancestor of *Tyrannosaurus rex*
Dilong

Dilong was also the ancestor of *Tyrannosaurus rex*. Like *Guanlong*, it was also feathered. Two features stood out: its tail had a cluster of feathers on the tip, like the tail of a lion; and above its eyes, it had feathers that looked like eyebrows! Because these ancestors had feathers, many researchers speculate that their descendant, *Tyrannosaurus rex*, was also feathered.

Though not as fierce as its descendant, *Dilong* was still capable of catching small mammals.

The world's most ferocious dinosaur
Tyrannosaurus rex

A large number of herbivores in present-day North America are walking along a dried up riverbed as they migrate to the north. Food has become more and more scarce, no longer enough for them to survive. Suddenly, a *Tyrannosaurus rex* emerges from a distant jungle; it notices a stray adult *Triceratops*. This makes the world's most ferocious dinosaur very excited; it hastens, attacks, and with its razor-edged teeth, it makes quick work of the big fellow. A *Quetzalcoatlus* is hovering above it; meanwhile, a *Dromaeosaurus* scurries back and forth around its feet. They are excited, anxiously waiting to eat some of its leftover scraps.

Tyrannosaurus rex

Body size: 12 meters in length
Diet: Carnivorous
Period of existence: Cretaceous
Fossil origin: United States, North America

5m

5m

Compsognathus
The dinosaur with a very beautiful jaw!

The emerald green forest is eerily silent, and a beam of lovely warm sunshine casts a long shadow on the figure of a *Compsognathus*. It stands there motion-less; in its line of sight, there is a *Bavarisaurus*, the *Compsognathus*'s favorite food. The small dinosaur gobbles up the lizard with no effort. Something as easy as this is no challenge for the *Compsognathus*.

Compsognathus

Body size: 1.4 meters in length
Diet: Carnivorous
Period of existence: Jurassic
Fossil origin: Germany, France, Europe

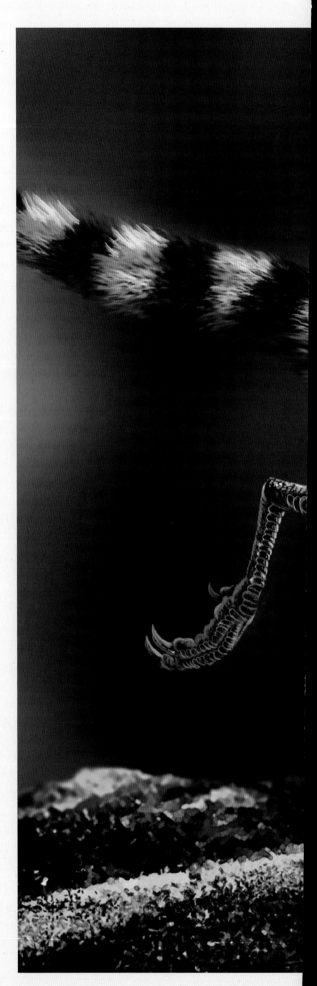

The beautiful
Sinocalliopteryx
and its unforgiving jaws

The *Sinocalliopteryx* is like the wicked witch queen from Snow White; it is beautiful but cruel. Look, a 2.37-meter-long *Sinocalliopteryx* is busy hunting a *Dromaeosaurus*. It is about to devour the latter's right leg whole inside its fearsome jaws.

In fact, nothing is wrong with the *Sinocalliopteryx* being vicious. To survive in such a harsh environment, keeping your stomach full is the first priority.

Sinocalliopteryx

Body size: 2.37 meters in length
Diet: Carnivorous
Period of existence: Cretaceous
Fossil origin: China, Asia

Sinosauropteryx

Body size: length of 0.9–2 meters

Diet: Carnivorous

Period of existence: Cretaceous

Fossil origin: China, Asia

50cm

50cm

I've seen those colors before
Sinosauropteryx

Kids, do you know what color dinosaurs were? Hey, don't cheat by peeking at the paintings! Most of the dinosaurs in this book have been painted by a talented artist. However, because we don't have any pictures of those dinosaurs, they are not necessarily colored like they were in real life. Let me tell you a secret, we know about the color of the *Sinosauropteryx*. This is because when its preserved fossil was discovered, it contained traces of melanosomes. Scientists analyzed them and found what color the *Sinosauropteryx* would have been when it was alive. So, the *Sinosauropteryx* you see in this picture is exactly the same color as the one that really existed.

A feathered dinosaur
Beipiaosaurus

The *Beipiaosaurus* looks very special. It is not covered in scales like most; instead, its body is covered with feathers. It was roughly 2.2 meters long, and it was considered to be the largest feathered dinosaur for a long period of time. However, in 2012 the *Yutyrannus huali* of the *Tyrannosaurus* family was discovered and took this honor away from the *Beipiaosaurus*. Nevertheless, at the time when it was discovered, it was a great shock to the scientific community. This is why its full given name is *Beipiaosaurus inexpectus*, which means "*Beipiaosaurus* the accident."

Beipiaosaurus

Body size: Approximately 2.2 meters in length
Diet: Herbivorous
Period of existence: Cretaceous
Fossil origin: China, Asia

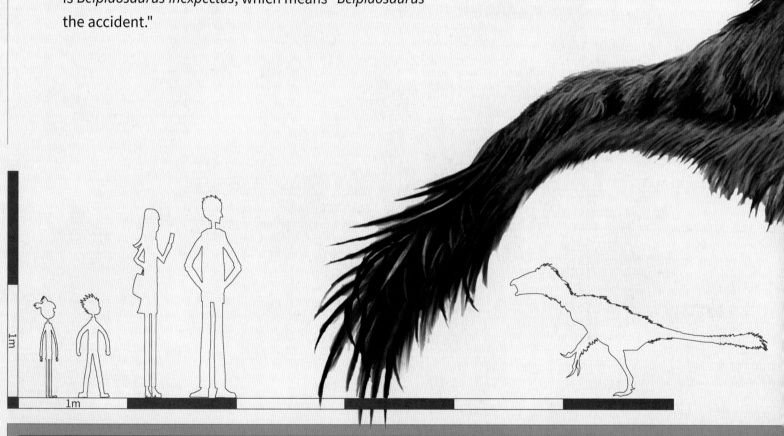

Millions of Years Ago	252.17 ±0.06	~247.2	~237		201.3 ±0.2		174.1 ±1.0	163 ±1
Epoch	Early Triassic	Middle Triassic	Late Triassic			Early Jurassic		Middle Jurassic
Period		Triassic				Jurassic		
Era								
Eon								

145.0   100.5   66.0

Early Cretaceous   Late Cretaceous

Cretaceous

It is like a big ostrich
Archaeornithomimus

The *Archaeornithomimus* must have been a part of a thriving family during the Early Cretaceous period because they account for a large part of the dinosaur fossils found today. An *Archaeornithomimus* looks like a big ostrich; it is tall and thin, covered with feathers, and it runs very fast. It mainly fed on insects and small animals, and occasionally ate various types of fruit.

Archaeornithomimus

Body size: Approximately 3.3 meters in length

Diet: Omnivorous

Period of existence: Cretaceous

Fossil origin: China, Uzbekistan, Asia

5m

5m

Mononykus
Its claw looks so lonely!

The *Mononykus* is a strange-looking dino-saur. It has a huge and weird-looking claw on each of its forelimbs. Do you know what that claw is for? Well, it is a difficult question. Scientists believe that this claw may have been used to dig up termites, just like an anteater. If this is true, then it is very likely that the *Mononykus* loved eating termites.

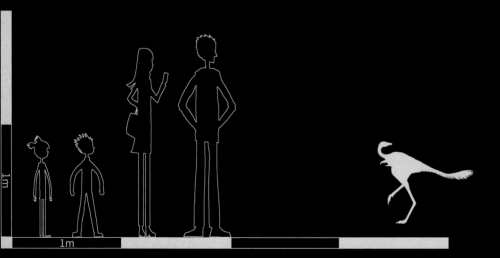

1m

Millions of Years Ago	252.17 ±0.06	~247.2	~237		201.3 ±0.2		174.1 ±1.0	163. ±1.
Epoch	Early Triassic	Middle Triassic	Late Triassic			Early Jurassic		Middle Jurassic
Period			Triassic				Jurassic	
Era								
Eon								

Mononykus

Body size: Approximately 1 meter in length

Diet: Omnivorous

Period of existence: Cretaceous

Fossil origin: Mongolia, Asia

~145.0

100.5

66.0

Late Jurassic

Late Cretaceous

Cretaceous

Mesozoic

Phanerozoic Eon

One of the smallest dinosaurs
Hesperonychus

The *Hesperonychus* loved to eat meat. However, they were much less dominating than the other carnivorous dinosaurs; they were even as small as a magpie. They are widely considered to have been the smallest dinosaurs. Of course, there are lots of advantages to being small. For example, if the *Hesperonychus* were able to catch a small lizard, it would have enough food for a long time, and it could easily run underneath the feet of giant sauropods without them even noticing!

Hesperonychus

Body size: 0.7 meters in length
Diet: Carnivorous
Period of existence: Cretaceous
Fossil origin: Canada, North America

1m

1m

The little fairy with four wings
Microraptor

Microraptor was the most unusual dinosaur. This small dinosaur had four wings. Even modern birds do not look like them. They were the first flying dinosaurs to be discovered. They were mediocre flyers and could only glide through the woods, but they were already miraculous among terrestrial dinosaurs. Look at this proud *Microraptor*. Before sunrise, it was flapping its wings, flying from the top of a tree, and starting its hunt!

Microraptor

Body size: 0.55–0.77 meters in length
Diet: Carnivorous
Period of existence: Cretaceous
Fossil origin: China, Asia

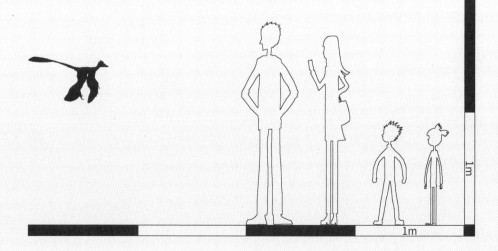

1m

Buitreraptors
hunting a
Gasparinisaura

A lovely *Gasparinisaura* is eating some tasty ferns with relish. The food looks fresh, with droplets of morning dew gleaming on the leaves. All herbivorous dinosaurs love eating ferns. However, three *Buitreraptors* have discovered the *Gasparinisaura*. They quietly surround it from behind, but the poor *Gasparinisaura* has no idea. Oh, a gruesome fight is about to start!

Buitreraptor

Body size: 1 meter in length
Diet: Carnivorous
Period of existence: Cretaceous
Fossil origin: Argentina, South America

Gasparinisaura

Body size: Approximately 1.7 meters in length
Diet: Herbivorous
Period of existence: Cretaceous
Fossil origin: Argentina, South America

Deinonychus
and its pair of scary-looking claws

The *Deinonychus*'s name means "terrifying claws," referring to the sharp, curved claws on its hind limbs. They clearly show that this dinosaur is a member of the *Dromaeosauridae* family; during battles, its sharp claws are able to pierce the skin of its enemies easily, ruthlessly making short work of them. Besides, it has an even more powerful weapon– high intelligence. It can come up with many different ways to deal with its enemies. The *Deinonychus* love to attacks in groups, and they will attack together in great numbers and share the prey with each other. One such group action produces enough food for many days! Now, they are charging towards their prey with their bloodthirsty mouths wide open, ready to strike.

Deinonychus

Body size: 3 meters in length

Diet: Carnivorous

Period of existence: Cretaceous

Fossil origin: United States, North America

The perfect hunter
Utahraptor

Utahraptor's forty-centimeter-long, sharp, sickle-like claws dove into the belly of *Cedrorestes*, who howled and tried to dodge the surprise attack. But it was too late. *Utahraptor* pulled out its claw and charged again. This time, its claws were pouncing on the *Cedrorestes*'s back. As *Cedrorestes* cried in despair, *Utahraptor*'s drool was dripping into the blood on its victim's back.

All dromaeosaurids were great predators, but even among them, the large, powerful, and armed *Utahraptor* was the perfect hunter.

Utahraptor

Size: 5.5 meters in length

Diet: Carnivorous

Period of existence: Cretaceous

Fossil origin: United States, North America

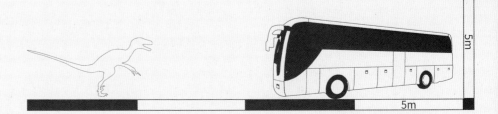

5m

5m

The crafty hunter
Velociraptor

Do you know who the most intelligent dinosaur among all dinosaurs is? Maybe you think it is the *Tyrannosaurus rex*, the *Stegosaurus*, or the *Allosaurus*. Well, it is none of these! All right, let me tell you, it is the *Velociraptor*, without a doubt. Although the *Velociraptors* were not as intelligent as humans, they were certainly smarter than horses or cattle! On silent nights they would spend their time thinking about fighting strategies. They loved to come up with new, clever tactics for hunting and dealing with their enemies. When facing strong enemies, because of their intelligence, they seldom lost!

Velociraptor

Body size: 1.8 meters in length
Diet: Carnivorous
Period of existence: Cretaceous
Fossil origin: Mongolia, China, Asia

Flapping its wings like a bird
Sinornithosaurus

You are familiar with birds that flap their wings. It is a common scene but a crucial step in flying. Have you ever seen a dinosaur flapping its wings?

Sinornithosaurus could do that. Its shoulder girdle was similar to a bird's, so its forelegs could stretch forward and up like a bird. But the feathered *Sinornithosaurus* could not fly, because its feathers were still primitive.

Sinornithosaurus

Body size: 1 meter in length

Diet: Carnivorous

Period of existence: Cretaceous

Fossil origin: China, Asia

1m

1m

The silent hunter
Luanchuanraptor

It was early morning in present-day Henan, China, during the Cretaceous period. The forest was so quiet that the only sound that could be heard is that of a stream rushing against its rubbled banks. Two *Luanchuanraptors* crept across a tree branch lying in the water, as they did not want to disturb the small lizard resting peacefully on the branch. Suddenly, a gust of air stirred up the leaves. The little lizard turned its head around to take a look. It was terrified to see the *Luanchuanraptors* and the gleaming claws on their hind limbs, not expecting the *Luanchuanraptors* would wake up so early. It tried to run away, but it slipped and fell off from the branch, right into the mouth of one of the hunters!

Luanchuanraptor

Body size: 2.6 meters in length
Diet: Carnivorous
Period of existence: Cretaceous
Fossil origin: China, Asia

The little dinosaur with short arms
Tianyuraptor

Although the forelimbs of the *Tianyuraptor* are so short that its friends laugh at them, this doesn't discourage it. It knows that its short forelimbs will never be strong enough to support flying, so it trains its hind limbs every day to become an excellent runner. It wants to run as fast as flying! Right now, it is pursuing those little grasshoppers and crickets lying on the tree branches with its lightning-fast speed. Its friends won't make fun of it again!

Tianyuraptor

Body size: 1.5 to 2 meters in length

Diet: Carnivorous

Period of existence: Cretaceous

Fossil origin: China, Asia

A real team worker
Dromaeosauroides

The *Dromaeosauroides* is an aggressive fighter. It is only between two and three meters long, but it is always picking fights against much bigger fellows. Look, these three *Dromaeosauroides* have picked a *Camptosaurus*; this is going to be three little puppies trying to take down an elephant. However, they are not afraid, thanks to the secret weapons on their hind limbs—sharp, terrifying claws. They are already on the attack, using their claws to tear into the skin of the *Camptosaurus*!

Dromaeosauroides

Body size: 2 to 3 meters in length
Diet: Carnivorous
Period of existence: Cretaceous
Fossil origin: Denmark, Europe

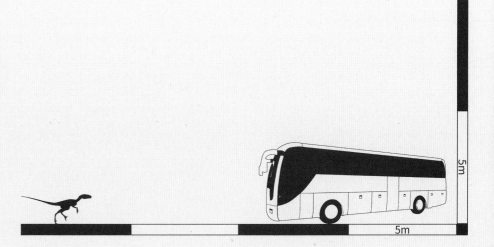

5m

5m

Dromaeosaurus

Body size: 2 meters in length

Diet: Carnivorous

Period of existence: Cretaceous

Fossil origin: Canada, United States, North America

1m

1m

Millions of Years Ago	252.17 ±0.06	~247.2	~237		201.3 ±0.2		174.1 ±1.0	163 ±1
Epoch	Early Triassic	Middle Triassic	Late Triassic			Jurassic	Middle Jurassic	
Period		Triassic					Jurassic	
Era								
Eon								

Working together
to kill their enemies
Dromaeosaurus

The *Dromaeosaurus* is very clever. Each *Dromaeosaurus* is very powerful on its own, but they usually prefer to act together with a few friends. They use their collective intelligence and strength to defeat their enemies. "Attacking in mass" was a sound strategy in their period; their group hunting adventures were nearly always successful!

~145.0   100.5   66.0

Late Jurassic   Early Cretaceous   Late Cretaceous

Cretaceous

Mesozoic

Phanerozoic Eon

Oviraptor
wasn't stealing eggs

The strange thing about the *Oviraptor* isn't its appearance but how it was discovered and named. When scientists found the *Oviraptor*'s fossil, its posture looked as if it was stealing another dinosaur's eggs. Because of this, scientists gave it the name meaning "egg-stealing dinosaur." Later on, scientists were surprised to discover that the *Oviraptor* was actually protecting its own children from being stolen by other dinosaurs. The *Oviraptor* wasn't a thief at all; it was actually a responsible parent! Nevertheless, once a dinosaur has a name, it can't be changed, so now the *Oviraptor* has to keep this bad name.

Oviraptor

Body size: 1.8–2.5 meters in length

Diet: Omnivorous

Period of existence: Cretaceous

Fossil origin: Mongolia, China, Asia

The magical feathers of the
Caudipteryx

Do you know what feathers are? A bird must have feathers to fly! However, what does that have to do with dinosaurs? Hah, this may be a big surprise to you, but some dinosaurs also had feathers! Have you seen the beautiful feathers covering the wings and tail of a *Caudipteryx*? Even though it had feathers, the *Caudipteryx* certainly couldn't fly as well as modern-day birds. The feathers were long on the tail, but too short on the wings. So they were mainly used to strut. Even so, it's still pretty impressive, right?

Caudipteryx

Body size: Approximately 0.7 meters in length

Diet: Omnivorous

Period of existence: Cretaceous

Fossil origin: China, Asia

Armed with both speed and power
The killer
Gigantoraptor

Most members of the *Oviraptoridae* family are small little things, but the *Gigantoraptor* is an exception. It is an enormous dinosaur, easily matching the mighty *Tyrannosaurus rex*. But it is more surprising to know that it is the dinosaur most closely related to birds. Its long limbs and upright body are very similar to that of modern-day birds. These attributes allow it to move with great speed and power. It must be very difficult to imagine what this gigantic "bird" looks like!

Gigantoraptor

Body size: 8 meters in length

Diet: Carnivorous

Period of existence: Cretaceous

Fossil origin: China, Asia

5m

5m

The Epidendrosaurus

What is it digging?

The *Epidendrosaurus* loves eating meat, but you would never guess that from its size. The most unique thing about this little guy is its long fingers. Look, its enormous eyes seem to have discovered something delicious, as it is using its long fingers to dig a treat out from that hole in a tree trunk! What could that snack be? Now I am really curious! Hey, stay with me and watch it digging!

Epidendrosaurus

Body size: Unknown
Diet: Carnivore and insectivore
Period of existence: Jurassic
Fossil origin: China, Asia

50cm

50cm

Epidexipteryx

It can spread its tail feathers open just like a peacock!

Have you ever seen a peacock showing off its tail feathers at the zoo? Well, let me tell you something: there was a dinosaur that had tail feathers just like the beautiful peacock. I am talking about the beautiful *Epidexipteryx*. Have you seen its tail? Doesn't it look just like a peacock fanning its tail feathers? Unlike the peacock, the *Epidexipteryx*'s "fan" is its tail, whereas the peacock's is made up of feathers on its back. The *Epidexipteryx* was very small, about the same size as a dove. Although it had beautiful feathers, it had the same shortcoming as the *Caudipteryx*—it couldn't fly!

Epidexipteryx

Body size: Approximately 0.45 meters in length
Diet: Omnivorous
Period of existence: Jurassic
Fossil origin: China, Asia

50cm

50cm

Lufengosaurus
Who's chasing me?

The weather is lovely and sunny, and the scent of fresh leaves mingles with the air. A *Lufengosaurus* lazily stretches, getting ready to go out for a walk. It is not particularly hungry because its stomach is full of its favorite leaves. Ever since the rains arrived, the leaves have multiplied and become plentiful. Just as the *Lufengosaurus* feels contented, suddenly it hears a burst of rapid footsteps coming from behind. The *Lufengosaurus* quickly turns around to see what is going on. It dares not be careless. Although it is six meters in length, it has a clumsy, heavy body and a gentle personality. It has no chance of fighting back against any fearsome predators!

Lufengosaurus

Body size: Approximately 5–8 meters in length
Diet: Herbivorous
Period of existence: Jurassic
Fossil origin: China, Asia

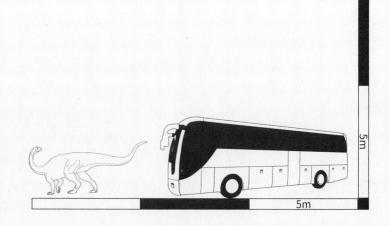

5m

5m

Plateosaurus
The dinosaur with feline claws

The *Plateosaurus* is a rather ordinary dinosaur. Its neck is neither long nor short, its tail is not particularly thick or thin, and its body is neither very large nor very small, so it is not very easy to recognize! However, if you really think so, then you must have overlooked its unique feature—the claws. The *Plateosaurus* has five claws on each of its front limbs, which are as sharp as the claws of a cat. Using these claws, it can cut any dinosaurs that try to attack it, and the *Plateosaurus* can also use its claws to gather leaves from trees. So, the claws are very useful indeed!

Plateosaurus

Body size: 4.8–10 meters in length
Diet: Herbivorous
Period of existence: Triassic
Fossil origin: Germany, Switzerland, Europe

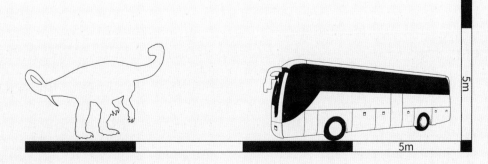

5m

5m

Doubtful largest dinosaur
Amphicoelias

Many dinosaurs were large, but which one was the biggest? Many people thought it was the *Amphicoelias*. One species, *A. fragillimus*, was thought to be fifty to sixty meters long, incredibly long even among dinosaurs. However, its size was based on a single fossil only, which mysteriously disappeared shortly after scientists studied it. The lack of evidence made *Amphicoelias*'s claim to be the largest doubtful. The other species, *Amphicoelias altus*, was only twenty-five to thirty meters long.

Amphicoelias

Body size: 25–30 meters in length

Diet: Herbivorous

Period of existence: Jurassic

Fossil origin: United States, North America

25m

25m

The longest animal on land
Diplodocus

Compared with the *Amphicoelias*, the *Diplodocus* had much better exposure. Many *Diplodocus* fossils have been discovered, and plenty of research has been done to understand this dinosaur.

The *Diplodocus* had a huge body, and it was one of the largest animals that ever lived on land, but despite its long body, it is very light. Do you know why? The reason is that its long, thin neck and tail accounted for most of its body length! Although the *Diplodocus*'s neck was very long, it could not bend easily, so it was limited in movement. Its long tail, which was much more flexible, could swing from side to side like a big whip and be used as a defensive weapon; if any of its enemies came close, it could swing its tail to drive them away.

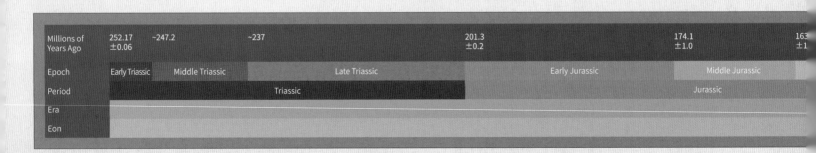

Millions of Years Ago	252.17 ±0.06	~247.2	~237		201.3 ±0.2		174.1 ±1.0	163 ±1
Epoch	Early Triassic	Middle Triassic	Late Triassic			Early Jurassic		Middle Jurassic
Period			Triassic				Jurassic	
Era								
Eon								

Diplodocus

Size: 25–35 meters in length

Diet: Herbivorous

Period of existence: Jurassic

Fossil origin: United States, North America

25m

25m

~145.0   100.5   66.0

Late Jurassic   Early Cretaceous   Late Cretaceous

Cretaceous

Mesozoic

Phanerozoic Eon

A little thing getting kicked around
Europasaurus

The word to describe the *Europoasaurus* is small. Even though it was part of the sauropods, the *Europasaurus* was like a little dwarf among giants. Scientists believe that the reason for that was that it lived on an isolated island, where there was not enough space or adequate food. To adapt to this life, it had no choice other than to become smaller in size. However, although it was tiny, it still retained the most obvious features of the sauropods, such as a long neck and a whip-like tail.

Europasaurus

Body size: 1.7–6.2 meters in length

Diet: Herbivorous

Period of existence: Jurassic

Fossil origin: Germany, Europe

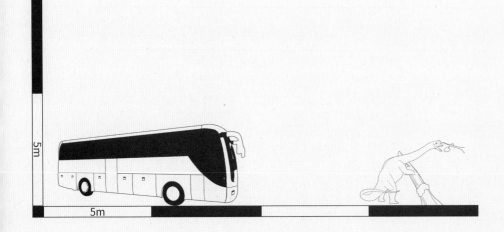

The tallest dinosaur
Sauroposeidon

There are lots of good things about being tall; at the very least, you can grab the tasty leaves on the top of trees. Three poor *Camptosaurus* on the ground wish that they could become taller. Their bellies are growling with hunger, but all they can do is to look enviously at the *Sauroposeidon* munching on fresh leaves. All leaves are too high for them to reach.

The *Sauroposeidon* is the world's tallest dinosaur. It is at least seventeen meters in height, which is about six stories high. Look, it is merrily munching away and laughing!

Sauroposeidon

Body size: Approximately 17 meters in height

Diet: Herbivorous

Period of existence: Cretaceous

Fossil origin: United States, North America

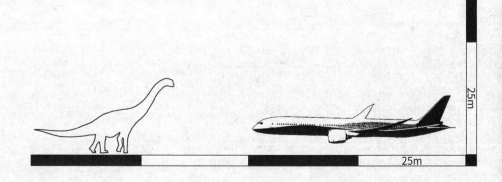

25m

25m

A dinosaur with feet like discs
Euhelopus

The feet of the *Euhelopus* look just like giant round discs, and its four limbs are like thick, sturdy columns. The *Euhelopus*'s neck is very long, being one of the longest necks out of all the sauropods. Its body is powerful, its front limbs are longer than the hind ones, and its long neck works in the same way as the neck of the giraffes, helping it reach food in the highest places.

Euhelopus

Body size: Approximately 15 meters in length

Diet: Herbivorous

Period of existence: Cretaceous

Fossil origin: China, Asia

Mamenchisaurus

Part of its body is like a long bridge

You can find a long bridge on the *Mamenchisaurus*. It has a slight curve, with one end of the bridge being its head and the other being its torso. Ha, if you haven't yet guessed, I am talking about the *Mamenchisaurus*'s neck. Judging by the neck's size relative to its body, the *Mamenchisaurus* has the longest neck out of all animals on Earth. It is between eighteen to thirty-four meters in length, half of which is its neck.

Mamenchisaurus

Size: 18–34 meters in length
Diet: Herbivorous
Period of existence: Jurassic
Fossil origin: China, Asia

It is content with being an ordinary dinosaur
Omeisaurus

25m

25m

The *Omeisaurus* seems to be an ordinary dinosaur. It doesn't appear to be special in any way; it has a long neck and a long tail just like the other sauropods. It is gentle and peaceful. None of this bothers the *Omeisaurus*, as this dinosaur prefers being normal. The *Omeisaurus* doesn't feel disappointed about not being special. On the contrary, dinosaurs like the *Omeisaurus* led pleasant lives, their families flourished, and the *Omeisaurus* became the most common sauropod dinosaur in modern-day China during the Jurassic period.

Omeisaurus

Body size: 10–20 meters in length
Diet: Herbivorous
Period of existence: Jurassic
Fossil origin: China, Asia

Shunosaurus

Its tail has a secret weapon!

Even though the *Shunosaurus* is considered a large sauropod dinosaur, its body is not particularly large. It is about as large as an adult female elephant, and its neck is a little shorter than the other sauropods. However, the *Shunosaurus* has something that most of the other sauropods can only dream about. At the end of its long tail, it has a club which looks like a peanut. This is its secret weapon to attack its enemies with!

Shunosaurus

Body size: 8–12 meters in length
Diet: Herbivorous
Period of existence: Jurassic
Fossil origin: China, Asia

5m

5m

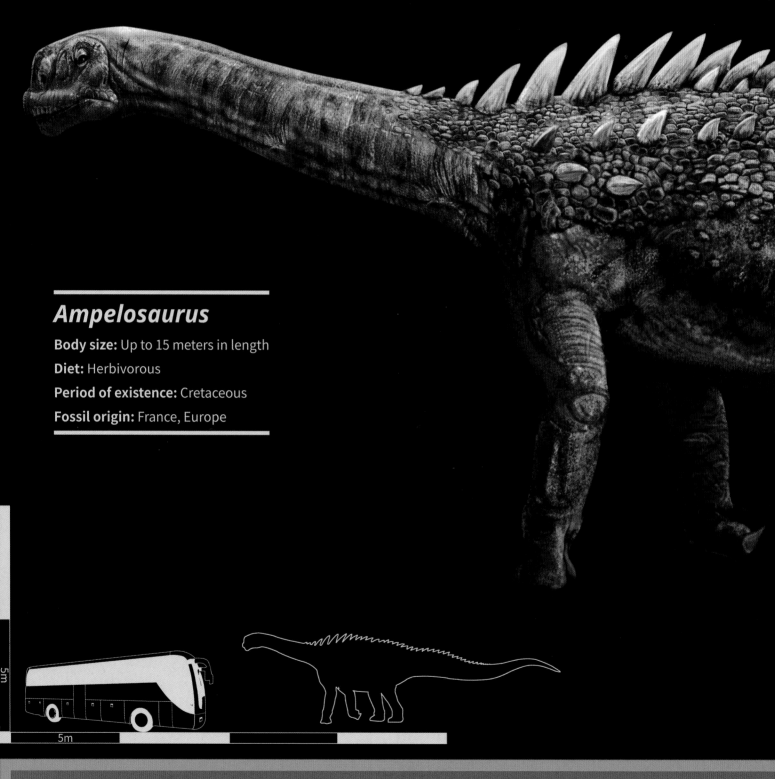

Ampelosaurus

Body size: Up to 15 meters in length

Diet: Herbivorous

Period of existence: Cretaceous

Fossil origin: France, Europe

5m

5m

Millions of Years Ago	252.17 ±0.06	~247.2	~237		201.3 ±0.2		174.1 ±1.0	163 ±1
Epoch	Early Triassic	Middle Triassic		Late Triassic		Early Jurassic		Middle Jurassic
Period			Triassic				Jurassic	
Era								
Eon								

Its body is covered with "grapes"
Ampelosaurus

The *Ampelosaurus* was discovered by scientists in a vineyard in the south of France; therefore, its name means "vine dragon." However, this name also describes the appearance of the *Ampelosaurus* very well. Why? Well, its back is entirely covered in rough, bumpy scales which look like bunches of grapes. The *Ampelosaurus* has a long neck, but it is not very flexible and can only move slightly from side to side. It has a long tail, four thick and stout limbs, and it is fond of eating fresh plants.

~145.0	100.5	66.0
Late Jurassic	Early Cretaceous	Late Cretaceous
	Cretaceous	
Mesozoic		
Phanerozoic Eon		

Dongyangosaurus
Where is the best place to give birth to a baby?

In every breeding season, all dinosaurs spend a great amount of time choosing a suitable place—the temperature can't be too low, and the soil can't be too hard. These conditions make it more likely that the eggs will hatch successfully. Right now, a *Dongyangosaurus* is looking for a suitable place, but once it arrives at the river bank, it realizes that the area is already crowded with others looking for a place to make their nests. This *Dongyangosaurus* decides it is better to search elsewhere, as it is not worth getting into a fight with its own family members over a nesting place!

Dongyangosaurus

Body size: Approximately 16 meters in length

Diet: Herbivorous

Period of existence: Cretaceous

Fossil origin: China, Asia

Daxiatitan

Body size: Approximately 26 meters in length

Diet: Herbivorous

Period of existence: Cretaceous

Fossil origin: China, Asia

25m

25m

The big fellow walking around with feet turned out
Daxiatitan

The *Daxiatitan* is a large fellow, very similar to the *Euhelopus*. However, this giant is not terrifying, but rather cute. It loves walking around with its feet turned out and bottom swaying from side to side, which looks so funny! However, you shouldn't try to copy it; it doesn't look very nice when children walk around with their feet turned out!

The chubbiest dinosaur of the dinosaur world
Huanghetitan

The *Huanghetitan* is one of the most famous fatties in the dinosaur world. It is known as the "King of Asia." Its body is about eighteen meters long—its toes are twenty centimeters in length. Its butt is 2.8 meters wide, which can be hugged by two or three kids with arms fully stretched out. Of course, its appetite is just as huge as its body. Look, these two *Huanghetitans* in the picture have already devoured all of the leaves in their territory, leaving the trees bare. To find more food, they must move to a more distant place!

Huanghetitan

Body size: Approximately 18 meters in length

Diet: Herbivorous

Period of existence: Cretaceous

Fossil origin: China, Asia

Argentinosaurus
Used to be world's largest

For a long time, *Argentinosaurus* was considered the world's largest dinosaur. Unlike *Amphicoelias*, which had only one missing fossil, *Argentinosaurus* had enough fossils for us to confirm that it was thirty-three to thirty-eight meters long and weighed seventy-three tons. These amazing numbers made it the largest dinosaur for a long time, until the discovery of *Ruyangosaurus*, which lived in present-day China in the Cretaceous period. Later, the honor of the biggest dinosaur was passed on from *Ruyangosaurus* to *Patagotitan*.

Millions of Years Ago	252.17 ±0.06	~247.2	~237		201.3 ±0.2		1 ±1.0	163 ±1
Epoch	Early Triassic	Middle Triassic	Late Triassic			Early Jurassic		Middle Jurassic
Period				Triassic			Jurassic	
Era								
Eon								

Argentinosaurus

Body size: 33–38 meters in length

Diet: Herbivorous

Period of existence: Cretaceous

Fossil origin: Argentina, South America

25m

25m

~145.0   100.5   66.0

Late Jurassic   Early Cretaceous   Late Cretaceous

Cretaceous

Mesozoic

Phanerozoic Eon

Origins of Ornithischian Fossils

Compiled by: PNSO

133 | *Jintasaurus*
Fossil Origin: China, Asia

134 | *Jinzhousaurus*
Fossil Origin: China, Asia

139 | *Altirhinus*
Fossil Origin: Mongolia, Asia

142 | *Tsintaosaurus*
Fossil Origin: China, Asia

148 | *Shantungosaurus*
Fossil Origin: China, Asia

152 | *Mandschurosaurus*
Fossil Origin: China, Asia

166 | *Yinlong*
Fossil Origin: China, Asia

170 | *Archaeoceratops*
Fossil Origin: China, Asia

172 | *Psittacosaurus*
Fossil Origin: Mongolia, China, Asia

174 | *Sinoceratops*
Fossil Origin: China, Asia

184 | *Tatisaurus*
Fossil Origin: China, Asia

187 | *Huayangosaurus*
Fossil Origin: China, Asia

193 | *Gigantspinosaurus*
Fossil Origin: China, Asia

195 | *Tuojiangosaurus*
Fossil Origin: China, Asia

197 | *Wuerhosaurus*
Fossil Origin: China, Asia

207 | *Saichania*
Fossil Origin: China, Asia

209 | *Zhongyuansaurus*
Fossil Origin: China, Asia

130 | *Iguanodon*
Fossil Origin: Belgium, United Kingdom, Europe

145 | *Olorotitan*
Fossil Origin: Russia, Europe

191 | *Miragaia*
Fossil Origin: Portugal, Europe

200 | *Polacanthus*
Fossil Origin: United Kingdom, Europe

136 | *Ouranosaurus*
Fossil Origin: Niger, Africa

189 | *Kentrosaurus*
Fossil Origin: Tanzania, Africa

129 | *Dryosaurus*
Fossil Origin: United States, North America

140 | *Corythosaurus*
Fossil Origin: Canada, North America

146 | *Parasaurolophus*
Fossil Origin: Canada, United States, North America

151 | *Hadrosaurus*
Fossil Origin: United States, North America

155 | *Anatotitan*
Fossil Origin: United States, North America

157 | *Maiasaura*
Fossil Origin: Canada, United States, North America

158 | *Edmontosaurus*
Fossil Origin: Canada, United States, North America

160 | *Stegoceras*
Fossil Origin: Canada, United States, North America

162 | *Dracorex*
Fossil Origin: United States, North America

165 | *Pachycephalosaurus*
Fossil Origin: United States, North America

168 | *Leptoceratops*
Fossil Origin: Canada, United States, North America

176 | *Styracosaurus*
Fossil Origin: Canada, North America

178 | *Centrosaurus*
Fossil Origin: Canada, North America

181 | *Torosaurus*
Fossil Origin: United States, North America

182 | *Triceratops*
Fossil Origin: United States, North America

198 | *Stegosaurus*
Fossil Origin: United States, North America

202 | *Sauropelta*
Fossil Origin: United States, North America

211 | *Ankylosaurus*
Fossil Origin: United States, North America

204 | *Kunbarrasaurus*
Fossil Origin: Australia, Oceania

 Asia **South America** **Africa** **Europe**   **North America**   **Oceania**

Period of Existence of Ornithischian Fossils in the Mesozoic Era

Compiled by: PNSO

129	*Dryosaurus* — Jurassic Period	130	*Iguanodon* — Cretaceous Period

129 | *Dryosaurus*
Jurassic Period

166 | *Yinlong*
Jurassic Period

184 | *Tatisaurus*
Jurassic Period

187 | *Huayangosaurus*
Jurassic Period

189 | *Kentrosaurus*
Jurassic Period

191 | *Miragaia*
Jurassic Period

193 | *Gigantspinosaurus*
Jurassic Period

195 | *Tuojiangosaurus*
Jurassic Period

198 | *Stegosaurus*
Jurassic Period

130 | *Iguanodon*
Cretaceous Period

133 | *Jintasaurus*
Cretaceous Period

134 | *Jinzhousaurus*
Cretaceous Period

136 | *Ouranosaurus*
Cretaceous Period

139 | *Altirhinus*
Cretaceous Period

140 | *Corythosaurus*
Cretaceous Period

142 | *Tsintaosaurus*
Cretaceous Period

145 | *Olorotitan*
Cretaceous Period

146 | *Parasaurolophus*
Cretaceous Period

148 | *Shantungosaurus*
Cretaceous Period

151 | *Hadrosaurus*
Cretaceous Period

152 | *Mandschurosaurus*
Cretaceous Period

155 | *Anatotitan*
Cretaceous Period

157 | *Maiasaura*
Cretaceous Period

Millions of Years Ago	252.17 ±0.06	~247.2	~237		201.3 ±0.2		174.1 ±1.0	163 ±1
Epoch	Early Triassic	Middle Triassic	Late Triassic		Early Jurassic		Middle Jurassic	
Period			Triassic				Jurassic	
Era								
Eon								

158 *Edmontosaurus*
Cretaceous Period

160 *Stegoceras*
Cretaceous Period

162 *Dracorex*
Cretaceous Period

165 *Pachycephalosaurus*
Cretaceous Period

168 *Leptoceratops*
Cretaceous Period

170 *Archaeoceratops*
Cretaceous Period

172 *Psittacosaurus*
Cretaceous Period

174 *Sinoceratops*
Cretaceous Period

176 *Styracosaurus*
Cretaceous Period

178 *Centrosaurus*
Cretaceous Period

181 *Torosaurus*
Cretaceous Period

182 *Triceratops*
Cretaceous Period

197 *Wuerhosaurus*
Cretaceous Period

200 *Polacanthus*
Cretaceous Period

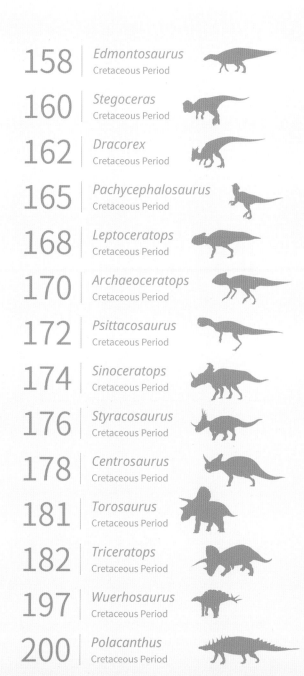

202 *Sauropelta*
Cretaceous Period

204 *Kunbarrasaurus*
Cretaceous Period

207 *Saichania*
Cretaceous Period

209 *Zhongyuansaurus*
Cretaceous Period

211 *Ankylosaurus*
Cretaceous Period

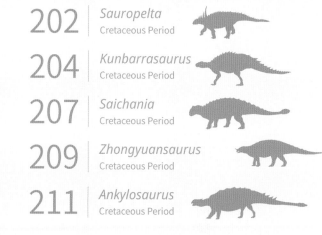

~145.0   100.5   66.0

Late Jurassic   Early Cretaceous   Late Cretaceous

Cretaceous

Mesozoic

hanerozoic Eon

A champion runner
Dryosaurus

The *Dryosaurus* was a herbivorous dinosaur. It would usually walk around on all four limbs; however, it could also often stand itself up on its hind limbs and run. The *Dryosaurus* practiced for a long time and became an excellent runner. When it faced an attack from a carnivorous dinosaur, it would use its speed to escape from danger! The *Dryosaurus* enjoyed a lively life, such as gathering food and playing together with many companions, and they would fight against their enemies together.

Dryosaurus

Body size: 2.4–4.3 meters in length
Diet: Herbivorous
Period of existence: Jurassic
Fossil origin: United States, North America

5m

5m

Iguanodon

Body size: 9–13 meters in length

Diet: Herbivorous

Period of existence: Cretaceous

Fossil origin: United Kingdom, Europe

One of the most famous dinosaurs
Iguanodon

The *Iguanodon* is very powerful with some "firsts." For example, scientists have discovered that it was the first dinosaur to have the ability to chew, which made it much easier to crush up leaves. Dr. Mantell, the scientist who discovered *Iguanodon*, reconstructed an image of the *Iguanodon*, which became the first reconstructed image of a dinosaur, an important development even though it was not very accurate. Moreover, two *Iguanodon* statues were erected outside the Crystal Palace in London, and they were the earliest full-scale models of dinosaurs. These bold attempts made the *Iguanodon* well known, and this act started people's understanding of what dinosaurs really looked like.

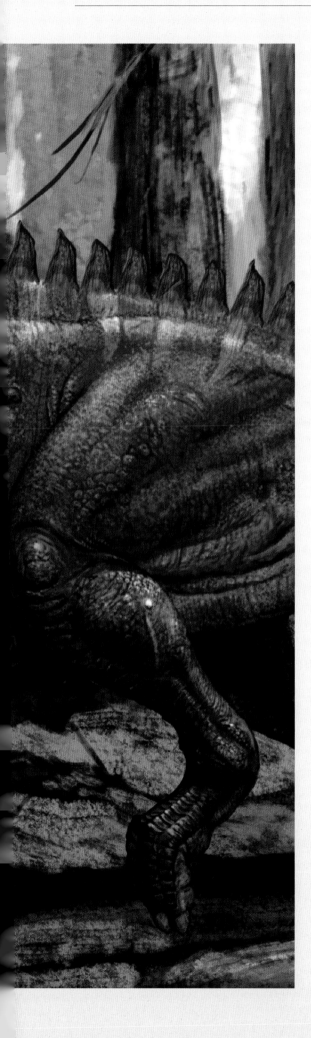

Jintasaurus
Its discovery suggests hadrosaurs might have originated in Asia

We all know that the *Iguanodon* and the *Hadrosauridae* family are very closely related. Both families belong to the Hadrosauriformes, with the former being more primitive. The *Jintasaurus* is similar to both the *Iguanodon* and hadrosaur in appearance, and it was a transition from the *Iguanodon* to the hadrosaur. The *Jintasaurus* lived in modern-day Gansu Province, China, during the Early Cretaceous period. Because of this discovery, scientists believe that the hadrosaur group most likely originated in Asia.

Jintasaurus

Body size: Approximately 6 meters in length
Diet: Herbivorous
Period of existence: Cretaceous
Fossil origin: China, Asia

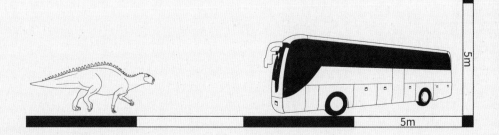

5m

5m

Its thumbs are similar to large thorns
Jinzhousaurus

The *Jinzhousaurus* fossil was well preserved when it was found by scientists, as its almost-complete body was kept on one large stone plate. Within the hadrosaur family, the *Jinzhousaurus* is particularly large. However, it has large nail-like digits on its forelimbs, and these can be used as a weapon against its enemies. The hind limbs of the *Jinzhousaurus* are strong, allowing it to move swiftly in the jungle!

Millions of Years Ago	252.17 ±0.06	~247.2	~237		201.3 ±0.2		174.1 ±1.0	163 ±1
Epoch	Early Triassic	Middle Triassic	Late Triassic		Early Jurassic		Middle Jurassic	
Period		Triassic				Jurassic		
Era								
Eon								

Jinzhousaurus

Body size: 7 meters in length

Diet: Herbivorous

Period of existence: Cretaceous

Fossil origin: China, Asia

5m

5m

~145.0

100.5

66.0

Late Jurassic

Early Cretaceous

Late Cretaceous

Cretaceous

Mesozoic

Phanerozoic Eon

The dinosaur with a "sail" on its back
Ouranosaurus

The *Ouranosaurus* has a "sail" on its back, which looks like a towering wall. This impressive-looking "sail" consists of muscle and tissue. It looks somewhat similar to the modern-day buffalo in North America. Scientists believe that the *Ouranosaurus* could use this sail to adjust its body temperature or store excess fat and water. Of course, it might also be a way for this tame fellow to scare away its enemies.

Millions of Years Ago	252.17 ±0.06	~247.2	~237		201.3 ±0.2		174.1 ±1.0	16: ±
Epoch	Early Triassic	Middle Triassic	Late Triassic		Early Jurassic		Middle Jurassic	
Period			Triassic			Jurassic		
Era								
Eon								

Ouranosaurus

Body size: 7 meters in length

Diet: Herbivorous

Period of existence: Cretaceous

Fossil origin: Niger, Africa

5m

5m

~145.0

100.5

66.0

Late Jurassic

ceous

Cretaceous

Late Cretaceous

Mesozoic

Phanerozoic Eon

Speaking with its big nose
Altirhinus

Altirhinus had a big and conspicuous nose. Some scientists believe that its big nose could make sounds to communicate with peers! Its forelegs were only half the length of the hind legs, so it walked on two feet most of the time. Like *Iguanodon*, *Altirhinus* also had a sharp first digit. This spike-like finger could break the hard shell of its favorite fruit or seed.

Altirhinus

Body size: 7-8 meters in length
Diet: Herbivorous
Period of existence: Cretaceous
Fossil origin: Mongolia, Asia

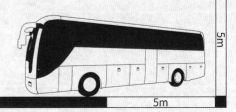

5m

5m

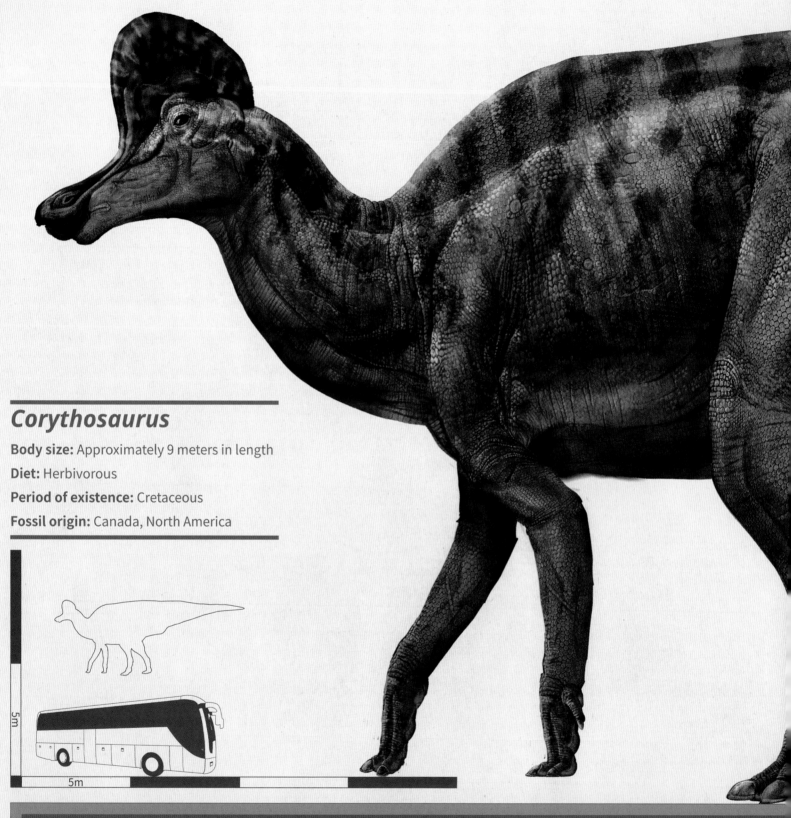

Corythosaurus

Body size: Approximately 9 meters in length

Diet: Herbivorous

Period of existence: Cretaceous

Fossil origin: Canada, North America

5m

5m

Millions of Years Ago	252.17 ±0.06	~247.2	~237		201.3 ±0.2		174.1 ±1.0	163 ±1
Epoch	Early Triassic	Middle Triassic	Late Triassic			Early Jurassic		Middle Jurassic
Period			Triassic				Jurassic	
Era								
Eon								

A crest that grows with age
Corythosaurus

The *Corythosaurus* had beautiful crowns of different sizes and shapes. Why weren't their crowns of the same size? Scientists believe that the reason is that the crown continues growing as the *Corythosaurus* ages. It is most likely that the crowns of male and female *Corythosaurus* were also different. The *Corythosaurus*'s crown was not only beautifully colored, but it could also make sounds. When many of them gathered, they would "play" lovely music just like an orchestra!

~145.0   100.5   66.0

Late Jurassic   Early Cretaceous   Late Cretaceous

Cretaceous

Mesozoic

Phanerozoic Eon

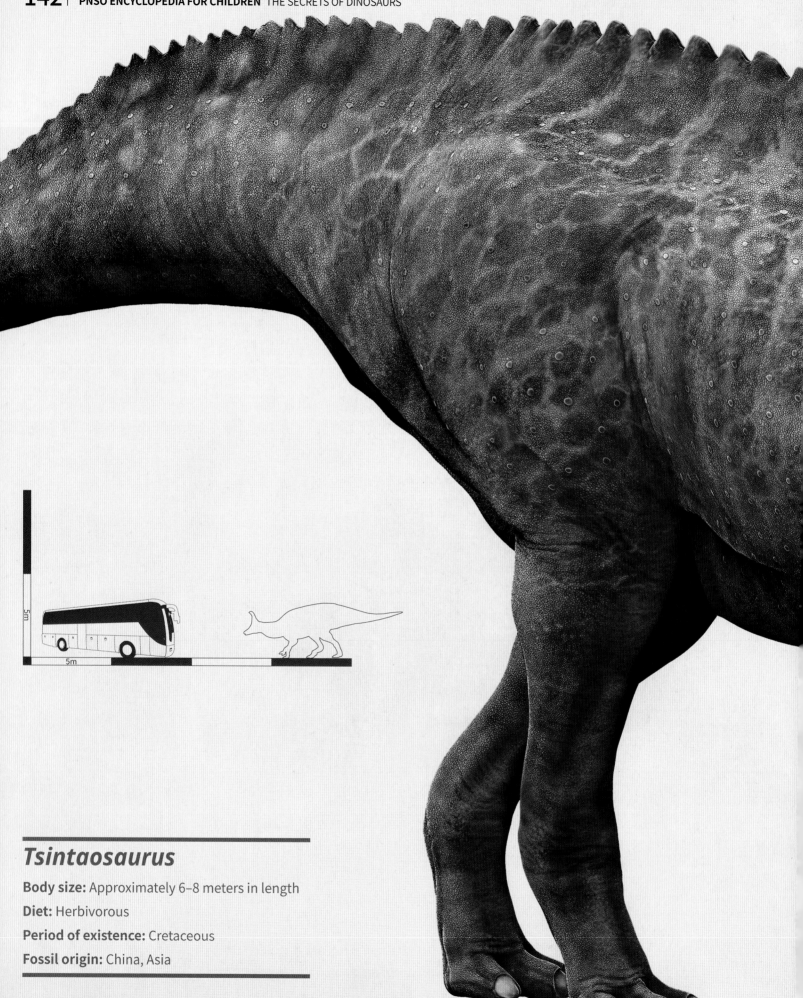

5m

5m

Tsintaosaurus

Body size: Approximately 6–8 meters in length

Diet: Herbivorous

Period of existence: Cretaceous

Fossil origin: China, Asia

Crested "duck"
Tsintaosaurus

Look at this one. You would think it is a duck by looking at its face alone. It had a flat and wide duck bill. But why did it have a crest and a gigantic body? How could a duck be so big? Of course, it was not a gigantic duck. It was *Tsintaosaurus*, a plant-eater.

Tsintaosaurus was a large hadrosaurid, and it could make sounds with its crest. This strong dinosaur usually walked on all fours.

A crest like a fan
Olorotitan

The *Olorotitan* is as large as a bus, with its unique feature being a strange-looking crest. The shape of its crest looks like an elaborate fan proudly spread open to attract others' attention. Its crest has a hollow part. Scientists believe that as air passes through that part, the crest makes loud sounds.

Olorotitan

Body size: 10–12 meters in length
Diet: Herbivorous
Period of existence: Cretaceous
Fossil origin: Russia, Europe

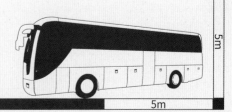

5m

5m

The dinosaur that sings
Parasaurolophus

Both the *Corythosaurus* and the *Olorotitan* use their crowns to make sounds, but to be honest, this is not all that special—many other members of the music-savvy *Hadrosauridae* family can do that. Look at the *Parasaurolophus*! It is also a member of the *Hadrosauridae* family. It can use its crown to create the most beautiful songs!

The *Parasaurolophus* has a hollow bone with a long chamber inside. When air passes through this chamber, it creates a variety of sounds! These sounds are only understood by its companions, acting like a secret language to communicate with each other.

Parasaurolophus

Body size: 10 meters in length

Diet: Herbivorous

Period of existence: Cretaceous

Fossil origin: Canada, United States, North America

5m

5m

Shantungosaurus

Body size: Approximately 15 meters in length

Diet: Herbivorous

Period of existence: Cretaceous

Fossil origin: China, Asia

The dinosaur fossil that was used to treat diseases
Shantungosaurus

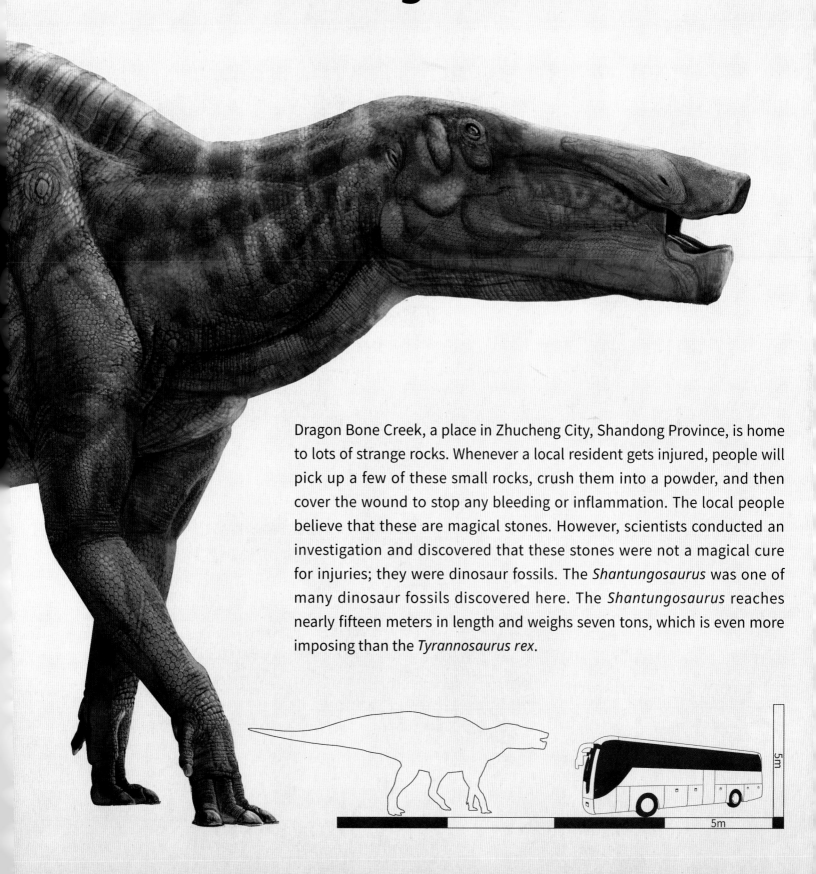

Dragon Bone Creek, a place in Zhucheng City, Shandong Province, is home to lots of strange rocks. Whenever a local resident gets injured, people will pick up a few of these small rocks, crush them into a powder, and then cover the wound to stop any bleeding or inflammation. The local people believe that these are magical stones. However, scientists conducted an investigation and discovered that these stones were not a magical cure for injuries; they were dinosaur fossils. The *Shantungosaurus* was one of many dinosaur fossils discovered here. The *Shantungosaurus* reaches nearly fifteen meters in length and weighs seven tons, which is even more imposing than the *Tyrannosaurus rex*.

5m

5m

The dinosaur with the most teeth
Hadrosaurus

The large *Hadrosaurus* belongs to the *Hadrosauridae* family. Its most noticeable feature is its flat and broad beak, which looks similar to that of a duck. Inside its mouth are more than two thousand teeth, more than that of any other dinosaur. With such a large number of teeth, wouldn't it be a lot of trouble if one tooth breaks? Well, actually that is not a problem to be worried about. Its large number of teeth are arranged in neat order. If a tooth gets damaged, a new one immediately replaces it. The *Hadrosaurus* is extremely lucky, such that it never has to worry about losing too many teeth.

Hadrosaurus

Body size: 7–10 meters in length
Diet: Herbivorous
Period of existence: Cretaceous
Fossil origin: United States, North America

5m

5m

China's first dinosaur
Mandschurosaurus

The *Mandschurosaurus* was another large member of the *Hadrosauridae* family, with a fairly large head and a mouth which was long and flat, just like that of a duck. Its body was stout and strong with a very long tail. The hind limbs of the *Mandschurosaurus* were longer than its front limbs, but it still usually walked on all fours, just like most of the other hadrosaurs. The *Mandschurosaurus* may not seem particularly remarkable, but it was the earliest dinosaur to be discovered in China, so it has been called "China's first dinosaur"!

Mandschurosaurus

Body size: 8–10 meters in length

Diet: Herbivorous

Period of existence: Cretaceous

Fossil origin: China, Asia

5m

5m

A giant "duck"
Anatotitan

The *Anatotitan* is a member of the *Hadrosauridae* family, but the cute-looking flat beak makes it look more like a duck, a gigantic one!

Now, this oversized "duck" is in serious trouble as a ferocious carnivorous dinosaur is chasing it. The *Anatotitan* must try to run faster because the predator's drool is already dripping all over its body!

Anatotitan

Body size: 10–12 meters in length
Diet: Herbivorous
Period of existence: Cretaceous
Fossil origin: United States, North America

5m

5m

A responsible and caring parent
Maiasaura

The sunshine is so pleasant that the mother *Maiasaura* decides to let her children go outside and play. Of course, she must also place her unhatched eggs outside under the sunshine so that the babies will come out of their shells faster! The little *Maiasaura* gleefully jump out from the nest, laughing and shouting as they play; they don't worry about any dangers. They know their mother is the best parent in the dinosaur world. No matter what problems they face, their mother will be there to save them!

Maiasaura

Body size: 9 meters in length
Diet: Herbivorous
Period of existence: Cretaceous
Fossil origin: Canada, United States, North America

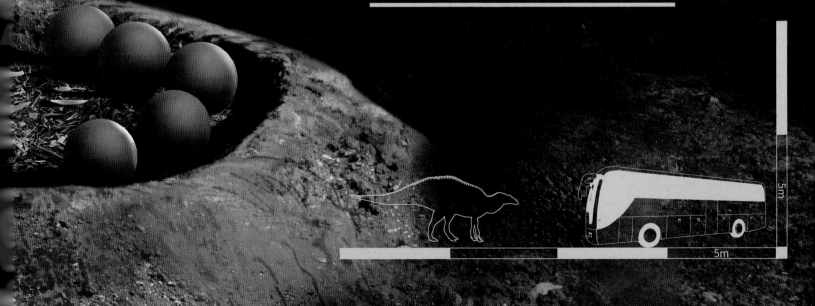

5m

5m

More than one thousand teeth
Edmontosaurus

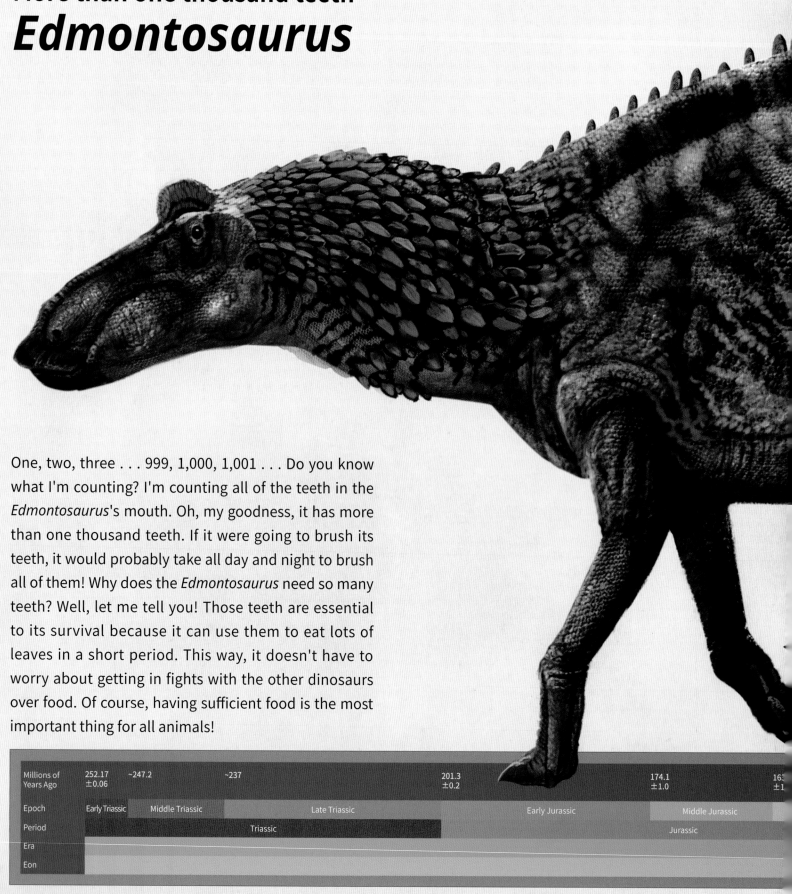

One, two, three . . . 999, 1,000, 1,001 . . . Do you know what I'm counting? I'm counting all of the teeth in the *Edmontosaurus*'s mouth. Oh, my goodness, it has more than one thousand teeth. If it were going to brush its teeth, it would probably take all day and night to brush all of them! Why does the *Edmontosaurus* need so many teeth? Well, let me tell you! Those teeth are essential to its survival because it can use them to eat lots of leaves in a short period. This way, it doesn't have to worry about getting in fights with the other dinosaurs over food. Of course, having sufficient food is the most important thing for all animals!

Millions of Years Ago	252.17 ±0.06	~247.2	~237		201.3 ±0.2		174.1 ±1.0	16: ±1
Epoch	Early Triassic	Middle Triassic	Late Triassic			Early Jurassic	Middle Jurassic	
Period			Triassic				Jurassic	
Era								
Eon								

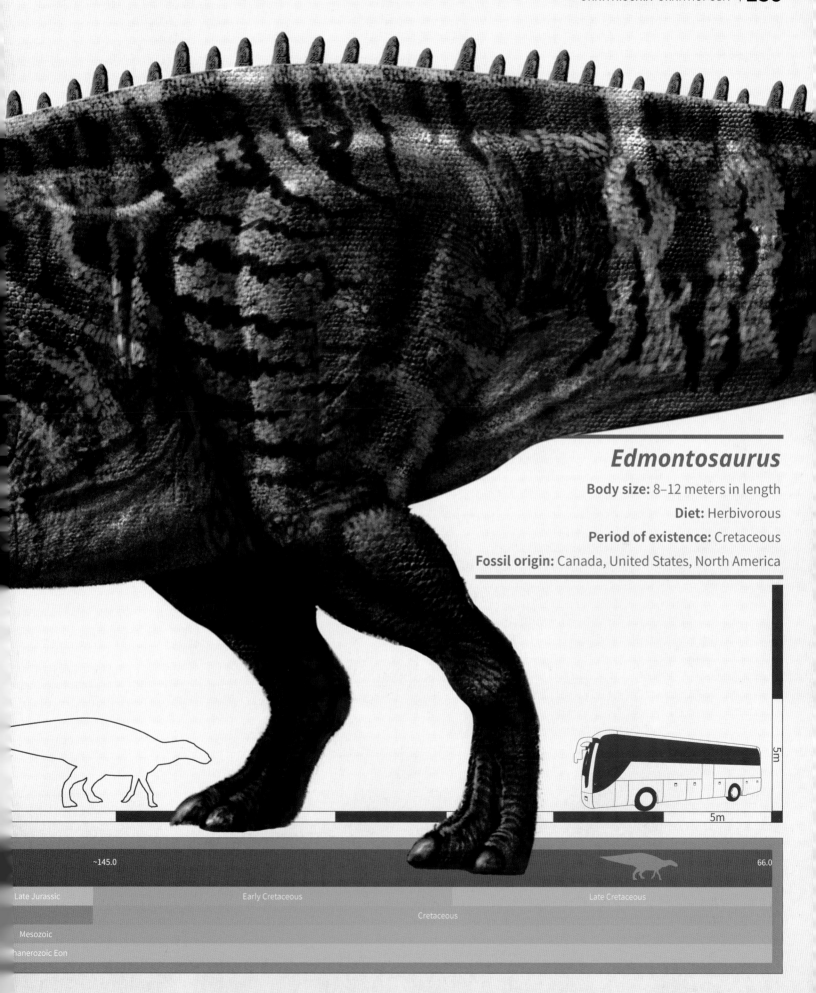

Edmontosaurus

Body size: 8–12 meters in length

Diet: Herbivorous

Period of existence: Cretaceous

Fossil origin: Canada, United States, North America

5m

5m

~145.0

66.0

Late Jurassic

Early Cretaceous

Late Cretaceous

Cretaceous

Mesozoic

Phanerozoic Eon

Millions of Years Ago	252.17 ±0.06	~247.2	~237		201.3 ±0.2		174.1 ±1.0	16 ±
Epoch	Early Triassic	Middle Triassic	Late Triassic		Early Jurassic		Middle Jurassic	
Period		Triassic				Jurassic		
Era								
Eon								

Always wearing a hat
Stegoceras

When you see the *Stegoceras*, do you feel that it is wearing a hat? It may seem so, but it is not a hat. Rather, it is a parietal bone, which is a common feature found among the pachycephalosaurs. The parietal bone in the *Stegoceras* is slightly different from others; it is not rough and bumpy, like those of its friends, but very smooth. The parietal bone of the *Stegoceras* is not very thick when it is born, but it thickens with age.

It is usually not easy to discover dinosaur fossils, but scientists were fortunate in finding the *Stegoceras* fossil intact. It is often used as a reference for reconstructing other family members.

Stegoceras

Body size: 2–2.5 meters in length

Diet: Herbivorous

Period of existence: Cretaceous

Fossil origin: Canada, United States, North America

~145.0   100.5   66.0

Late Jurassic   Early Cretaceous   Late Cretaceous

Cretaceous

Mesozoic

Phanerozoic Eon

A magical dinosaur
Dracorex

Have you seen the film *Harry Potter*? If you've seen it, surely you remember the Hogwarts School of Witchcraft and Wizardry. The *Dracorex*'s full name is "*Dracorex hogwartsia*," and as you can guess, its name is dedicated to the school. It is a magical-looking dinosaur, and you can see that from its head. On top of the *Dracorex*'s head, you find knots, horns, and a crown, all of which make it look like a magical creature. Of course, it doesn't really have any magical powers; it is just a clever fellow that enjoys eating plants.

5m

5m

Millions of Years Ago	252.17 ±0.06	~247.2	~237		201.3 ±0.2		174.1 ±1.0	16: ±
Epoch	Early Triassic	Middle Triassic	Late Triassic				Middle Jurassic	
Period			Triassic			ssic		
Era								
Eon								

Dracorex

Body size: 3–4 meters in length

Diet: Herbivorous

Period of existence: Cretaceous

Fossil origin: United States, North America

Late Jurassic

Early Cretaceous

Cretaceous

Late Cretaceous

66.0

Mesozoic

Phanerozoic Eon

The dinosaur with "bumps"
Pachycephalosaurus

The *Pachycephalosaurus* probably could never be called beautiful; its head and cheeks are covered with bone nodules and small spines, and even the dome of its head is surrounded with lots of sharp, thorny knurls. All of these things make its skin look rough and bumpy, like an ill person. However, the *Pachycephalosaurus* doesn't care one bit because all of these ugly-looking things help it control its body temperature, which is very useful!

Pachycephalosaurus

Body size: 4.5–6 meters in length

Diet: Herbivorous

Period of existence: Cretaceous

Fossil origin: United States, North America

5m

5m

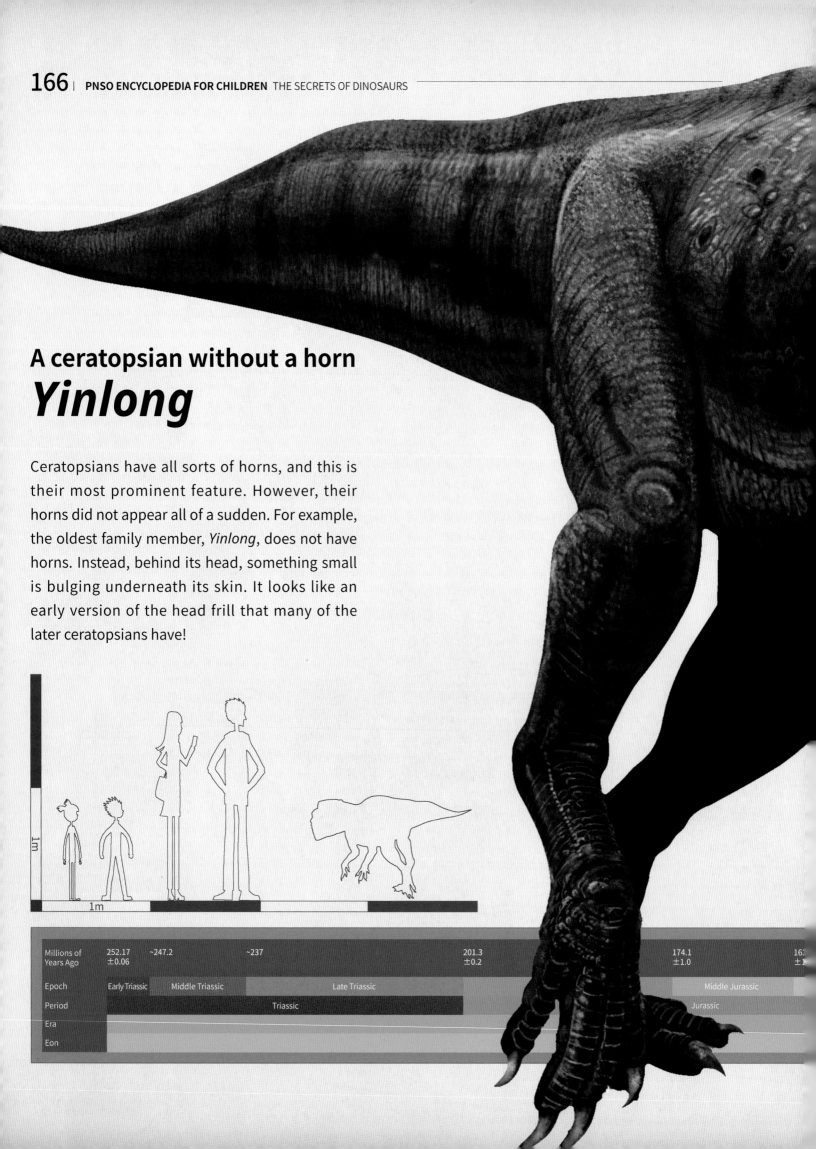

A ceratopsian without a horn
Yinlong

Ceratopsians have all sorts of horns, and this is their most prominent feature. However, their horns did not appear all of a sudden. For example, the oldest family member, *Yinlong*, does not have horns. Instead, behind its head, something small is bulging underneath its skin. It looks like an early version of the head frill that many of the later ceratopsians have!

1m

1m

Millions of Years Ago	252.17 ±0.06	~247.2	~237		201.3 ±0.2		174.1 ±1.0	16 ±
Epoch	Early Triassic	Middle Triassic	Late Triassic				Middle Jurassic	
Period			Triassic				Jurassic	
Era								
Eon								

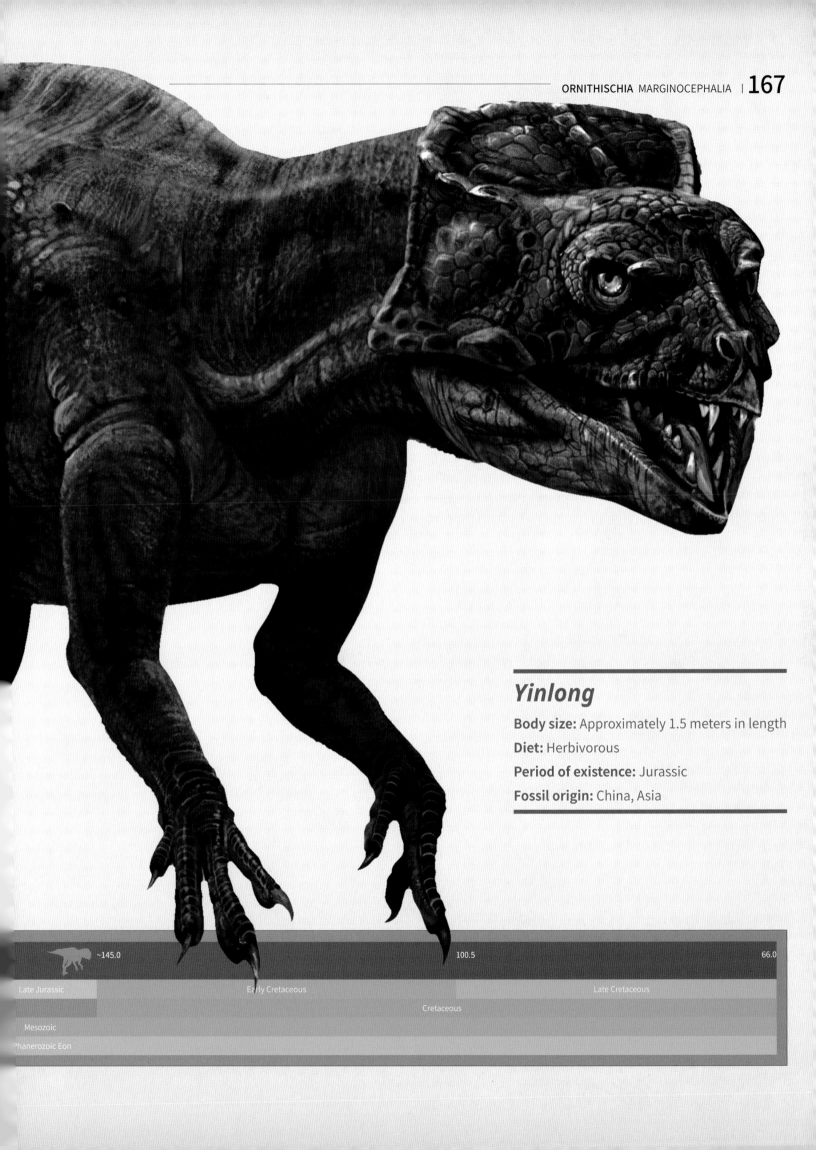

Yinlong

Body size: Approximately 1.5 meters in length

Diet: Herbivorous

Period of existence: Jurassic

Fossil origin: China, Asia

~145.0   100.5   66.0

Late Jurassic   Early Cretaceous   Late Cretaceous

Cretaceous

Mesozoic

Phanerozoic Eon

The North American
Leptoceratops
What a cute dinosaur

The *Leptoceratops* is a lovely little dinosaur that lived in North America. It is believed to be roughly two meters in length, tiny during that era when giants walked around Earth. The *Leptoceratops* was cute, with its large head and the little shield behind its head. It had a pair of bright eyes and a sharp beak just like that of a parrot. It could use its razor-sharp beak to tear apart broad leaves and needle-like leaves. Of course, the juicy flowering plants which appeared during that period were also lovely treats.

Leptoceratops

Body size: Approximately 2 meters in length
Diet: Herbivorous
Period of existence: Cretaceous
Fossil origin: Canada, United States, North America

1m

1m

Don't break my eggs!
Archaeoceratops

The *Archaeoceratops*'s babies are about to hatch, and it is excited about that. It brushes off layers of dried leaves covering the eggs to get more sunshine. However, at this moment a pterosaur suddenly swoops down and picks up one of the eggs, before roaring back up into the sky. This scares the *Archaeoceratops*, and it shrieks, "Don't break my egg!" The *Archaeoceratops* screams as loud as possible, but it is too late, her baby's eggshell has been cracked open!

Archaeoceratops

Body size: 1–1.5 meters in length

Diet: Herbivorous

Period of existence: Cretaceous

Fossil origin: China, Asia

With a mouth like that of a cute little parrot
Psittacosaurus

Even though the *Psittacosaurus* belongs to the ceratopsians, its most noticeable feature is not its horn but its mouth. It has a sharp beak which looks just like that of a parrot, so scientists have given it the name "parrot dinosaur." The *Psittacosaurus* is approximately two meters long, and it loves to eat fresh vegetables. The *Psittacosaurus* is a very caring and loving parent just like the *Maiasaura*. Look, right now this mother *Psittacosaurus* is playing with its children!

Psittacosaurus

Body size: Approximately 2 meters in length
Diet: Herbivorous
Period of existence: Cretaceous
Fossil origin: Mongolia, China, Asia

1m

1m

With many beautiful and formidable horns
Sinoceratops

The *Sinoceratops* is one of the most sturdy herbivores, with a body length of close to seven meters. However, its body strength and size are not its main weapons for keeping enemies away. The *Sinoceratops*'s horns are undoubtedly its most important weapon. The *Sinoceratops* has many long and beautiful horns, among which the most obvious one is the thick and hefty horn on its nose, which can reach more than thirty centimeters in length. That big horn acts like a guard for the *Sinoceratops*, warning all of its enemies, "Danger—don't get close!"

Millions of Years Ago	252.17 ±0.06	~247.2	~237		201.3 ±0.2		174.1 ±1.0	16: ±1
Epoch	Early Triassic	Middle Triassic	Late Triassic			Early Jurassic	Middle Jurassic	
Period			Triassic				Jurassic	
Era								
Eon								

Sinoceratops

Body size: 6–7 meters in length

Diet: Herbivorous

Period of existence: Cretaceous

Fossil origin: China, Asia

45.0 100.5 66.0

Late Cretaceous

Cretaceous

Mesozoic

Phanerozoic Eon

The dinosaur with the most horns
Styracosaurus

The *Styracosaurus* is a special ceratopsian; among all family members, it has the most horns. There is a pair of short horns on its forehead and a sharp horn on its nose. It has a head frill with two or three pairs of dangerous-looking horns, of which the longest can reach up to fifty-five centimeters. Adding to its collection are countless small horns lining its head frill. This horned and mighty "gladiator" scares away most of the predators.

5m

5m

Millions of Years Ago	252.17 ±0.06	~247.2	~237		201.3 ±0.2		174.1 ±1.0	16 ±
Epoch	Early Triassic	Middle Triassic	Late Triassic			Early Jurassic		Middle Jurassic
Period			Triassic					Jurassic
Era								
Eon								

Styracosaurus

Body size: 5.5–6 meters in length
Diet: Herbivorous
Period of existence: Cretaceous
Fossil origin: Canada, North America

Late Ju

Early Cretaceous

Late

66.0

The single-horned warrior
Centrosaurus

The most important feature of the *Centrosaurus* is the very long and sharp horn on its nose. Contrary to what you may think, the *Centrosaurus* has more than one horn; it has three horns, just like the *Triceratops*. The only difference is that its two other horns are rather short, whereas the one on its nose is massive! Also, some *Centrosaurus* have their horns curved forward, while others have them curved backward! The shape of their horns may differ slightly, but these can always be used as powerful weapons. With their horns, the *Centrosaurus* become a group of "single-horned warriors" within the *Ceratopsidae* family.

5m

5m

Centrosaurus

Body size: 6 meters in length
Diet: Herbivorous
Period of existence: Cretaceous
Fossil origin: Canada, North America

Torosaurus

Its head is equal to thirteen human heads in size

The nine-meter-long *Torosaurus* looks similar to a giant rhinoceros. It has four stout limbs and a sturdy body; however, it weighs far more than a rhinoceros! The most prominent feature of the *Torosaurus* is its enormous head; it is almost three meters long and of the size of thirteen of our own heads. That's one big head! However, the shield on the back of its head is rather unremarkable, much less decorated compared to many of the other members of the *Ceratopsidae* family. The *Torosaurus* eats a wide range of plants, including ferns, cycads, conifers, and many others.

Torosaurus

Body size: Approximately 9 meters in length
Diet: Herbivorous
Period of existence: Cretaceous
Fossil origin: United States, North America

5m

5m

The most famous member of the
Ceratopsidae family
Triceratops

Thanks to its might, the *Triceratops* is certainly the most famous member of the *Ceratopsidae* family. It is an enormous dinosaur, nearly nine meters long, three meters high, and weighing about six tons. Above its eyes are two horns, each more than one meter in length, and a very solid head frill, which is useful in fighting. The *Triceratops* is so good at defending itself that even the *Tyrannosaurus rex* does not find it an easy target. Nevertheless, the *Triceratops* also has cute body parts; for example, look at the little horn on its nose!

Triceratops

Body size: 7.9–9 meters in length

Diet: Herbivorous

Period of existence: Cretaceous

Fossil origin: United States, North America

5m

5m

Millions of Years Ago	252.17 ±0.06	~247.2	~237		201.3 ±0.2		174.1 ±1.0	163 ±1
Epoch	Early Triassic	Middle Triassic		Late Tr		Early Jurassic	Middle Jurassic	
Period			Triassic				Jurassic	
Era								
Eon								

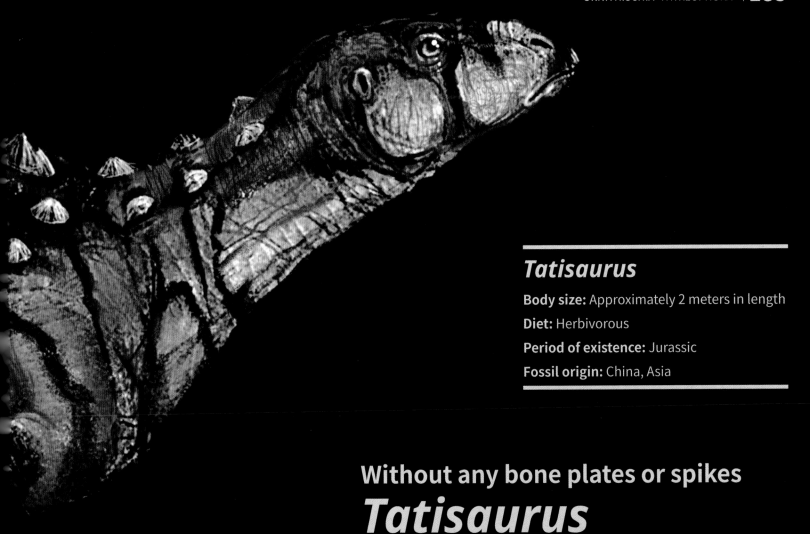

Tatisaurus

Body size: Approximately 2 meters in length
Diet: Herbivorous
Period of existence: Jurassic
Fossil origin: China, Asia

Without any bone plates or spikes
Tatisaurus

Although the *Tatisaurus* belongs to the same group from which the *Stegosaurus* originated, it does not have any of the bone plates which the family members are so proud of. Instead, it has small nodules, which look as if they might develop into bone plates but are not worth mentioning now! Nevertheless, the *Tatisaurus* is still remarkable because it was the first member of the thyreophorans. The rise of this new breed of mighty herbivores began with the *Tatisaurus*; soon afterward, the stegosaur family began to develop defensive weapons such as bone plates, spikes, and armored plates that could be used against those terrible carnivorous dinosaurs!

~145.0	100.5	66.0
Late Jurassic	Early Cretaceous	Late Cretaceous
	Cretaceous	
Mesozoic		
Phanerozoic Eon		

The dinosaur with the most bone plates on its back
Huayangosaurus

The stegosaur family members are well known for the formidable bone plates on their backs. Among which, the *Huayangosaurus* is famous for having the greatest number of them. Sixteen pairs of impressive bone plates stand symmetrically arranged along its back. In addition to those, two large spikes on its shoulders protect its shoulders and neck. The *Huayangosaurus* is one of the smaller dinosaurs in the stegosaur family, but thanks to all of its powerful weapons, it can easily handle the notorious predator in its local region—the *Gasosaurus*.

Huayangosaurus

Body size: 4.5 meters in length

Diet: Herbivorous

Period of existence: Jurassic

Fossil origin: China, Asia

5m

5m

Strange bony plates
Kentrosaurus

Kentrosaurus, a stegosaurian, was about five meters long, with a long, slender neck and longer hind limbs than forelegs. The bony plates on its back were unusual. The upper body had triangular plates, and these gradually thinned in the lower half, eventually becoming spines. These plates were not used in direct combat. They were more likely to scare predators. But the spikes on the tip of its tail were real fighting weapons.

Kentrosaurus

Body size: 5 meters in length
Diet: Herbivorous
Period of existence: Jurassic
Fossil origin: Tanzania, Africa

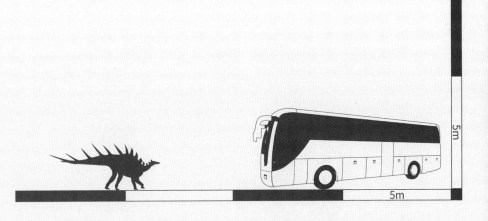

5m

5m

The long-necked
Miragaia

The stegosaur family are known for their short necks, with the *Miragaia* being an exception. Its neck is more than 1.8 meters long, yet its body is less than six meters. Such a neck-to-body ratio is higher than many long-necked sauropods. A long neck, of course, has many uses; the *Miragaia* is able to see very far, and it can easily munch on the leaves found on the top of the trees!

Miragaia

Body size: 5.5–6 meters in length

Diet: Herbivorous

Period of existence: Jurassic

Fossil origin: Portugal, Europe

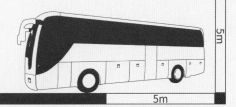

5m

5m

"General"
Gigantspinosaurus
It carries a sword on its shoulders

Most dignified generals carry their swords on their waists. However, the *Gigantspinosaurus* doesn't do that; it prefers to carry its sword on its shoulders. When it encounters a ferocious *Yangchuanosaurus*, and a battle begins, the "sword" which rests across its shoulders makes it look like a fearless general. Look, it is trying to use its "sword" to pierce through the *Yangchuanosaurus*'s flesh. The terrified cries of the *Yangchuanosaurus* are a testament to the power of the *Gigantspinosaurus*!

This "sword" is actually a collection of spines that rests across the shoulders of the *Gigantspinosaurus*. This is a fearsome weapon; the bone plates along its back and small spines that cover its tail form an indestructible weapon set that the *Gigantspinosaurus* uses mercilessly.

Gigantspinosaurus

Body size: 5.4 meters in length
Diet: Herbivorous
Period of existence: Jurassic
Fossil origin: China, Asia

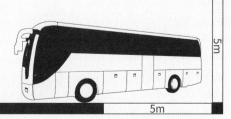

5m

5m

Its shoulder spikes stick straight up
Tuojiangosaurus

Hey, why are we looking at another fellow with spikes on its shoulders? Well, this dinosaur looks different from the *Gigantspinosaurus*, but its spikes seem more deadly, like a pair of swords sticking straight up towards the sky. I can't bear to imagine what would happen if some unlucky dinosaur were to hit on them head on!

This is the *Tuojiangosaurus*, it is one of the larger members of the stegosaur family. It has four sturdy limbs and enjoys eating low-hanging plants.

Tuojiangosaurus

Body size: 7.5 meters in length

Diet: Herbivorous

Period of existence: Jurassic

Fossil origin: China, Asia

5m

5m

Its back is covered with rectangular "toy bricks"
Wuerhosaurus

All stegosaurians had bony plates on their backs, but the shapes of these plates varied from one stegosaurian to another. Look at this *Wuerhosaurus*. While *Stegosaurus* had diamond-shaped plates, and *Dacentrurus* had nail-like ones, this *Wuerhosaurus* had rectangular ones. It looked like someone had put a lot of rectangular toy bricks on its back. Cute!

Wuerhosaurus

Body size: 7 meters in length
Diet: Herbivorous
Period of existence: Cretaceous
Fossil origin: China, Asia

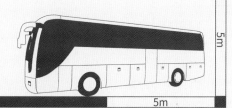

5m

5m

Most famous stegosaurian
Stegosaurus

You have probably never seen such a strange dinosaur. It had seventeen diamond-shaped bony plates on its back and four sharp, one-meter-long "spears" on the tip of its tail. The ground under those big feet trembled as they walked. What were they doing? Well, it seemed that they were going to eat some green leaves. Haha, don't be frightened by their appearance. These giants, *Stegosaurus*, were gentle herbivorous dinosaurs. Look at these two naughty *Dermodactylus*. They were taking a free ride by landing on one of these "nice guys"!

In general, *Stegosaurus* did not attack others. It would use the plates and the "spear" for defense only!

Stegosaurus

Body size: 7–9 meters in length

Diet: Herbivorous

Period of existence: Jurassic

Fossil origin: United States, North America

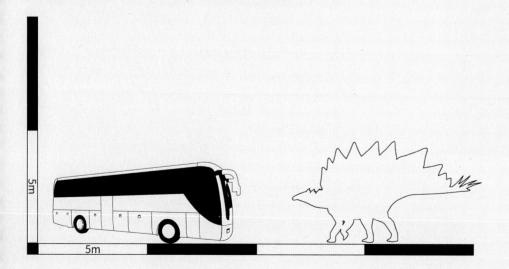

5m

5m

Polacanthus

Body size: 4–5 meters in length

Diet: Herbivorous

Period of existence: Cretaceous

Fossil origin: United Kingdom, Europe

5m

5m

Millions of Years Ago	252.17 ±0.06	~247.2	~237		1.3		174.1 ±1.0
Epoch	Early Triassic	Middle Triassic		Lat		Early Jurassic	Middle Jurassic
Period			Triassic				Jurassic
Era							
Eon							

Like an enormous hedgehog
Polacanthus

The *Polacanthus* is about four or five meters in length and looks remarkably similar to an enormous hedgehog with its body wrapped up tightly in spikes. Its hips have large bone plates that look like huge shields, while its neck and back are fitted with circular pieces of bone, and its tail has two rows of triangular spikes. When enemies attack, it will carefully observe the situation and shrewdly choose which weapons to fight with to defeat its enemies!

5.0   100.5   66.0

arly Cretaceous   Late Cretaceous

Cretaceous

Sauropelta

Body size: Approximately 5 meters in length

Diet: Herbivorous

Period of existence: Cretaceous

Fossil origin: United States, North America

Millions of Years Ago	252.17 ±0.06	~247.2	~237		201.3 ±0.2		174.1 ±1.0	163 ±1
Epoch	Early Triassic	Middle Triassic	Late Triassic			Early Jurassic	Middle Jurassic	
Period		Triassic					Jurassic	
Era								
Eon								

5m

5m

Sauropelta
It has a really long tail!

The *Sauropelta* is a member of the *Ankylosauridae*, which means that it has the family's signature set of equipment: its neck, back, and bottom are all covered in hard armored plates, while large spikes protrude from its sides. These weapons allow the *Sauropelta* to both defend itself and launch attacks against its enemies. However, the *Sauropelta* has something unique that its relatives lack: it has an extremely long tail that looks very stiff. It usually keeps its tail lifted high up in the air, waving it back and forth to frighten away enemies.

~145.0 100.5 66.0

Late Jurassic Early Cretaceous Late Cretaceous

Cretaceous

Mesozoic

hanerozoic Eon

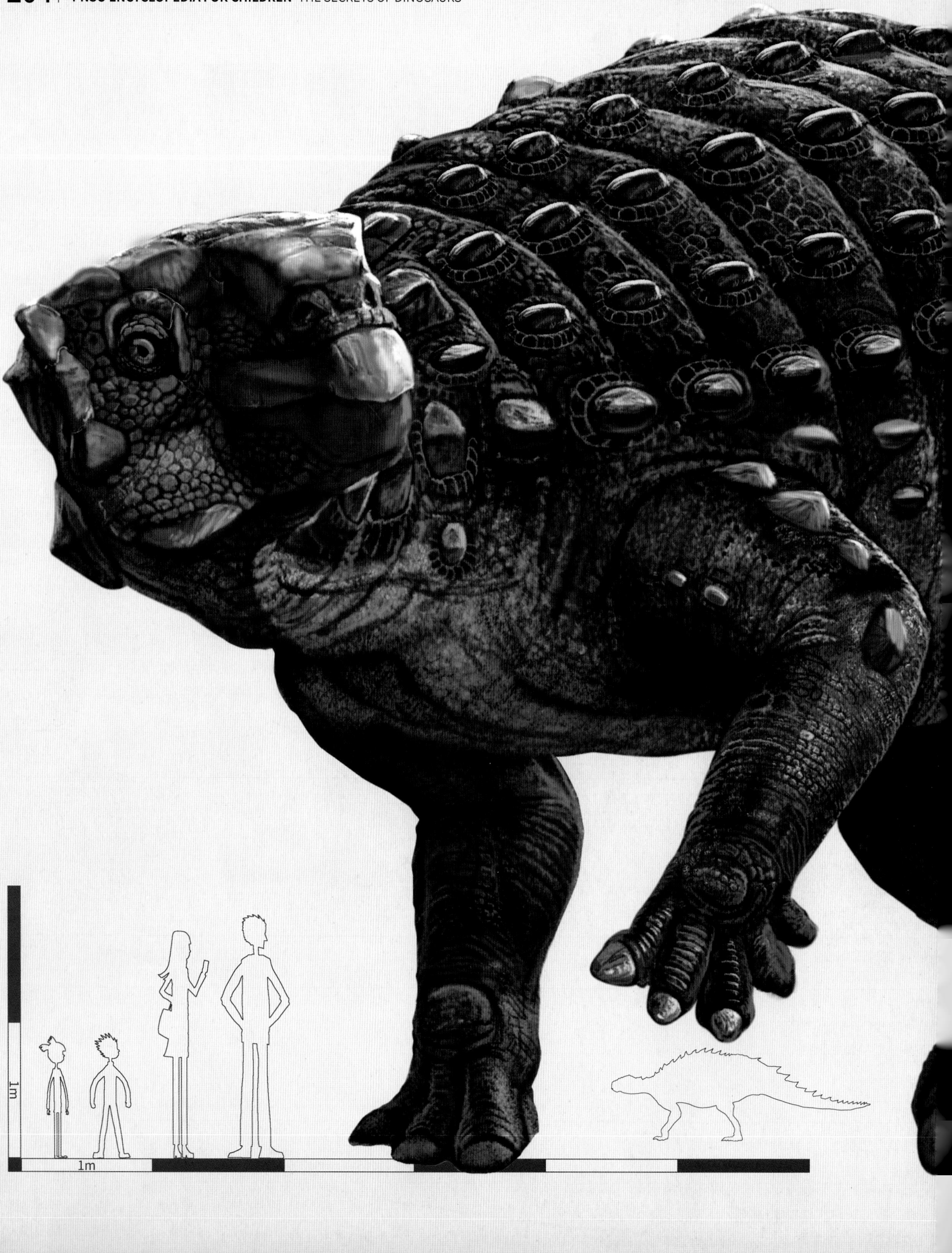
1m
1m

Australia's armored fighter
Kunbarrasaurus

One hundred fifteen million years ago in modern-day Australia, the weather was surprisingly pleasant, and a *Kunbarrasaurus*, approximately two meters in length, walked leisurely along the plains, searching for low-hanging ferns to munch on. It wasn't afraid whatsoever of an attack from any carnivorous dinosaur; its back was covered in rows of armored plates and bone spikes. It looked so fearsome that no one would dare to bully it!

Kunbarrasaurus

Body size: Approximately 2 meters in length
Diet: Herbivorous
Period of existence: Cretaceous
Fossil origin: Australia, Oceania

Perfect armor
Saichania

All ankylosaurians had armor that other dinosaurs envied. Within this group, other ankylosaurians probably envied *Saichania*. The name of *Saichania* means "beautiful fossil." But it was better known for its perfect armor! Its head, back, buttocks, tail, sides, and limbs all had bony plates or sharp spines. You would hardly find an exposed part on a *Saichania*. No wonder even the other armored ankylosaurians envied it!

Saichania

Body size: Approximately 7 meters in length
Diet: Herbivorous
Period of existence: Cretaceous
Fossil origin: Mongolia, Asia

5m

5m

Enjoying breakfast
Zhongyuansaurus

It is crisp and fresh in the morning. A *Zhongyuansaurus* can't wait to wake up from its dream and walk over to the pond to enjoy breakfast before the day warms up. When it arrives at the edge of the pond, it finds that two *Luanchuanraptors* have already made it there. Although they are rather agile carnivorous dinosaurs, the *Zhongyuansaurus*'s body is covered in armor and spikes, so it is not afraid. It comes over to them,

walking directly past and towards some low hanging ferns nearby. With its head lowered, it begins happily munching away in front of the *Luanchuanraptors*. With a body that is five meters in length and covered in armor, there is nothing that these tiny little carnivorous *Luanchuanraptors* can do to bother the *Zhongyuansaurus*!

Zhongyuansaurus

Body size: 5 meters in length

Diet: Herbivorous

Period of existence: Cretaceous

Fossil origin: China, Asia

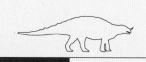

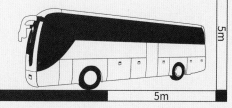

5m

5m

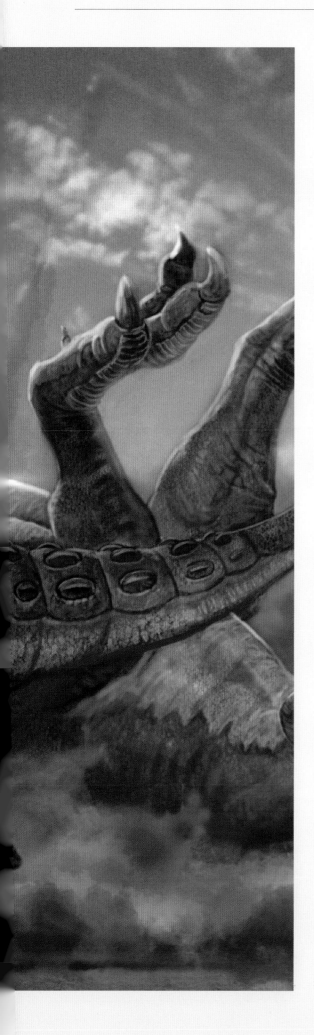

The armored warrior
Ankylosaurus

"Hey, don't run away, I'm just going to munch on these leaves!" Although the *Ankylosaurus* tries as hard as it can to explain, that carnivorous dinosaur busy hunting for small lizards is terrified and scurries away as fast as it can.

Oh, I suppose this little dinosaur can't be blamed for being afraid. Even though the *Ankylosaurus* is unquestionably a herbivorous dinosaur, it has a body that is entirely covered in armor, and a tail with an intimidating hammer on the end of it. Everyone remembers when it used that "hammer" to shatter the leg of the *Tyrannosaurus rex*. Now, no one dares to disturb the *Ankylosaurus*—they don't want to suffer a similar fate!

Ankylosaurus

Body size: Approximately 7 meters in length
Diet: Herbivorous
Period of existence: Cretaceous
Fossil origin: United States, North America

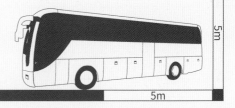

5m

5m

Index

A

Abelisaurus / 28

Allosaurus / 34

Australovenator / 41

Archaeornithomimus / 59

Amphicoelias / 99

Ampelosaurus / 114

Argentinosaurus / 122

Altirhinus / 139

Anatotitan / 155

Archaeoceratops / 170

Ankylosaurus / 211

B

Beipiaosaurus / 56

Buitreraptor / 67

C

Coelophysis / 24

Compsognathus / 50

Caudipteryx / 86

Corythosaurus / 140

Centrosaurus / 178

D

Dilophosaurus / 23

Dilong / 46

Deinonychus / 68

Dromaeosauroides / 81

Dromaeosaurus / 82

Diplodocus / 100

Dongyangosaurus / 116

Daxiatitan / 119

Dryosaurus / 129

Dracorex / 162

E

Epidendrosaurus / 91

Epidexipteryx / 92

Europasaurus / 102

Euhelopus / 107

Edmontosaurus / 158

F

G

Gasosaurus / 33

Giganotosaurus / 42

Guanlong / 44

Gasparinisaura / 67

Gigantoraptor / 89

Gigantspinosaurus / 193

H

Herrerasaurus / 21

Hesperonychus / 62

Huanghetitan / 120

Hadrosaurus / 151

Huayangosaurus / 187

I

Irritator / 15

Iguanodon / 130

J

Jintasaurus / 133

Jinzhousaurus / 134

K

Kentrosaurus / 189

Kunbarrasaurus / 204

L

Luanchuanraptor / 76

Lufengosaurus / 95

Leptoceratops／168

M

Monolophosaurus／12

Megalosaurus／19

Majungasaurus／26

Mononykus／60

Microraptor／65

Mamenchisaurus／108

Mandschurosaurus／152

Maiasaura／157

Miragaia／191

N

O

Oviraptor／84

Omeisaurus／110

Ouranosaurus／136

Olorotitan／145

P

Plateosaurus／97

Parasaurolophus／146

Pachycephalosaurus／165

Psittacosaurus／172

Polacanthus／200

Q

R

Rajasaurus／30

S

Spinosaurus／17

Szechuanosaurus／36

Sinocalliopteryx／53

Sinosauropteryx／54

Sinornithosaurus／74

Sauroposeidon／105

Shunosaurus／112

Shantungosaurus／148

Stegoceras／160

Sinoceratops／174

Styracosaurus／176

Sauropelta／202

Saichania／207

Stegosaurus／198

T

Tyrannosaurus／49

Tianyuraptor／78

Tsintaosaurus／142

Torosaurus／181

Triceratops／182

Tatisaurus／184

Tuojiangosaurus／195

U

Utahraptor／71

V

Velociraptor／73

W

Wuerhosaurus／197

X

Y

Yangchuanosaurus／38

Yinlong／166

Z

Zhongyuansaurus／209

References

1. Zhao, Xi-Jin, and Philip J. Currie. 2010. "A large crested theropod from the Jurassic of Xinjiang, People's Republic of China." *Canadian Journal of Earth Sciences* 30: 2027–36.

2. Zhao, Xijin, Roger B. J. Benson, Stephen L. Brusatte, and Philip J. Currie. 2010. "The postcranial skeleton of *Monolophosaurus jiangi* (Dinosauria: Theropoda) from the Middle Jurassic of Xinjiang, China, and a review of Middle Jurassic Chinese theropods." *Geological Magazine* 147 (1): 13–27.

3. Buffetaut, E., and M. Ouaja. 2002. "A new specimen of *Spinosaurus* (Dinosauria, Theropoda) from the Lower Cretaceous of Tunisia, with remarks on the evolutionary history of the *Spinosauridae.*" *Bulletin de la Société Géologique de France* 173 (5): 415.

4. Sereno, P. C., A. L. Beck, D. B. Dutheil, B. Gado, H. C. E. Larsson, G. H. Lyon, J. D. Marcot, O. W. M. Rauhut, R. W. Sadleir, C. A. Sidor, D. D. Varricchio, G. P. Wilson, and J. A. Wilson. 1998. "A long-snouted predatory dinosaur from Africa and the evolution of spinosaurids." *Science* 282: 1298–1302.

5. Sereno, P. C., D. B. Dutheil, M. Larochene, H. C. A. Larsson, G. H. Lyon, P. M. Magwene, C. A. Sidor, D. J. Varricchio, and J. A. Wilson. 1996. "Predatory dinosaurs from the Sahara and Late Cretaceous faunal differentiation." *Science* 272 (5264): 986–91.

6. Smith, J. B., M. C. Lamanna, K. J. Lacovara, P. Dodson, J. R. Smith, J. C. Poole, R. Giegengack, and Y. Attia. 2001. "A giant sauropod dinosaur from an Upper Cretaceous mangrove deposit in Egypt." *Science* 292 (5522): 1704–6.

7. Galton, P. M. 1985. "The poposaurid thecodontian *Teratosaurus suevicus* von Meyer, plus referred specimens mostly based on prosauropod dinosaurs." *Stuttgarter Beitrage zur Naturkunde* Serie B 116: 1–29.

8. Sereno, P. C., and F. E. Novas. 1992. "The complete skull and skeleton of an early dinosaur." *Science* 258 (5085): 1137–40.

9. Nesbitt, S. J., N. D. Smith, R. B. Irmis, A. H. Turner, A. Downs, and M. A. Norell. 2009. "A complete skeleton of a Late Triassic saurischian and the early evolution of dinosaurs." *Science* 326 (5959): 1530–33.

10. Ezcurra, M. D. 2010. "A new early dinosaur (Saurischia: Sauropodomorpha) from the Late Triassic of Argentina: a reassessment of dinosaur origin and phylogeny." *Journal of Systematic Palaeontology* 8 (3): 371–425.

11. Welles, S. P. 1954. "New Jurassic dinosaur from the Kayenta formation of Arizona." *Bulletin of the Geological Society of America* 65: 591–98.

12. Nesbitt, S. J., A. H. Turner, G. M. Erickson, and M. A. Norell. 2006. "Prey choice and cannibalistic behaviour in the theropod *Coelophys.*" *Biology Letters* 2 (4): 611–14.

13. Agnolin, F. L., and P. Chiarelli. 2010. "The position of the claws in *Noasauridae* (Dinosauria: Abelisauroidea) and its implications for abelisauroid manus evolution." *Paläontologische Zeitschrift* 84: 293–300.

14. Sues, Hans-Dieter, and Phillipe Taquet. 1979. "A pachycephalosaurid dinosaur from Madagascar and a Laurasia-Gondwanaland connection in the Cretaceous." *Nature* 279 (5714): 633–35.

15. Makovicky, Peter J., Sebastián Apesteguía, and Federico L. Agnolín. 2005. "The earliest dromaeosaurid theropod from South America." *Nature* 437 (7061): 1007–11.

16. Sereno, P. C., J. A. Wilson, and J. L. Conrad. 2004. "New dinosaurs link southern landmasses in the Mid-Cretaceous." *Proceedings of the Royal Society of London: Biological Sciences* 271: 1325–30.

17. Sharma, N., R. K. Kar, A. Agarwal, and R. Kar. 2005. "Fungi in dinosaurian (*Isisaurus*) coprolites from the Lameta Formation (Maastrichtian) and its reflection on food habit and environment." *Micropaleontology* 51 (1): 73–82.

18. Dong, Z., and Z. Tang. 1985. "A new Mid-Jurassic theropod (*Gasosaurus constructus* gen et sp. nov.) from Dashanpu, Zigong, Sichuan Province, China." *Vertebrata PalAsiatica* 23 (1): 77–82.

19. Chure, Daniel J., and James H. Madsen. 1996. "On the presence of furculae in some non-maniraptoran theropods." *Journal of Vertebrate Paleontology* 16: 573–77.

20. Peng, G. Z., Y. Ye, Y. H. Gao, C. K. Shu, and S. Jiang. 2005. "Jurassic dinosaur faunas in Zigong." *Sichuan People's Publishing House* 236.

21. Carrano, M. T., R. B. J. Benson, and S. D. Sampson. 2012. "The phylogeny of Tetanurae (Dinosauria: Theropoda)." *Journal of Systematic Palaeontology* 10 (2): 211.

22. Dong, Zhiming, Yihong Zhang, Xuanmin Li, and Shiwu Zhou. 1978. "A new carnosaur from Yongchuan County, Sichuan Province." *Chinese Science Bulletin* 23 (5): 302–4.

23. Hocknull, Scott A., Matt A. White, Travis R. Tischler, Alex G. Cook, Naomi D. Calleja, Trish Sloan, and David A. Elliott. 2009. "New mid-Cretaceous (latest Albian) dinosaurs from Winton, Queensland, Australia." *PLoS ONE* 4 (7): e6190.

24. White, M. A., A. G. Cook, S. A. Hocknull, T. Sloan, G. H. K. Sinapius, and D. A. Elliott. 2012. "New Forearm Elements Discovered of Holotype Specimen *Australovenator wintonensis* from Winton, Queensland, Australia." *PLoS ONE* 7 (6): e39364.

25. Coria, R. A., and L. Salgado. 1995. "A new giant carnivorous dinosaur from the Cretaceous of Patagonia." *Nature* 377: 225–26.

26. Seebacher, F. 2001. "A new method to calculate allometric length-mass relationships of dinosaurs." *Journal of Vertebrate Paleontology* 21 (1): 51–60.

27. Xu, X., J. M. Clark, C. A. Forster, M. A. Norell, G. M. Erickson, D. A. Eberth, C. Jia, and Q. Zhao. 2006. "A basal tyrannosauroid dinosaur from the Late Jurassic of China." *Nature* 439: 715–18.

28. Xu, X., M. A. Norell, X. Kuang, X. Wang, Q. Zhao, and C. Jia. 2004. "Basal tyrannosauroids from China and evidence for protofeathers in tyrannosauroids." *Nature* 431: 680–84.

29. Turner, A. H., D. Pol, J. A. Clarke, G. M. Erickson, and M. A. Norell. 2007. "Supporting online material for: A basal dromaeosaurid and size evolution preceding avian flight." *Science* 317: 1378–81.

30. Ji, Q., P. J. Currie, M. A. Norell, and S. Ji. 1998. "Two feathered dinosaurs from northeastern China." *Nature* 39 3(6687): 753–61.

31. Brusatte, S. L., M. A. Norell, T. D. Carr, G. M. Erickson, J. R. Hutchinson, A. M. Balanoff, G. S. Bever, J. N. Choiniere, P. J. Makovicky, and X. Xu. 2010. "Tyrannosaur paleobiology: new research on ancient exemplar organisms." *Science* 329 (5998): 1481–85.

32. Therrien, F., and D. M. Henderson. 2007. "My theropod is bigger than yours . . . or not: estimating body size from skull length in theropods." *Journal of Vertebrate Paleontology* 27 (1): 108–15.

33. Xu, Xing. 2006. "Palaeontology: Scales, feathers and dinosaurs." *Nature* 440 (7082): 287–88.

34. Butler, R. J., and P. Upchurch. 2007. "Highly incomplete taxa and the phylogenetic relationships of the theropod dinosaur *Juravenator starki*." *Journal of Vertebrate Paleontology* 27 (1): 253–56.

35. Hwang, S. H., M. A. Norell, J. Qiang, and G. Keqin. 2004. "A large compsognathid from the Early Cretaceous Yixian Formation of China." *Journal of Systematic Paleontology* 2: 13–39.

36. Ji, S., Q. Ji, J. Lu, and C. Yuan. 2007. "A new giant compsognathid dinosaur with long filamentous integuments from Lower Cretaceous of Northeastern China." *Acta Geologica Sinica* 81 (1): 8–15.

37. Zhou, Z. 2006. "Evolutionary radiation of the Jehol Biota: chronological and ecological perspectives." *Geological Journal* 41: 377–93.

38. Xu, X., Z.-L. Tang, and X.-L. Wang. 1999. "A therizinosauroid dinosaur with integumentary structures from China." *Nature* 399: 350–54.

39. Suzuki, S., L. M. Chiappe, G. J. Dyke, M. Watabe, R. Barsbold, and K. Tsogtbaatar. 2002. "A new specimen of *Shuvuuia deserti* Chiappe et al., 1998 from the Mongolian Late Cretaceous with a discussion of the relationships of alvarezsaurids to other theropod dinosaurs." *Contributions in Science* 494: 1–18.

40. Chiappe, L. M., M. A. Norell, and J. M. Clark. 1998. "The skull of a relative of the stem-group bird *Mononykus*." *Nature* 392: 275–78.

41. Schweitzer, M. H., J. A. Watt, R. Avci, L. Knapp, L. Chiappe, M. A. Norell, and M. Marshall. 1999. "Beta-keratin specific immunological reactivity in feather-like structures of the Cretaceous alvarezsaurid, *Shuvuuia deserti*." *Journal of Experimental Zoology* Part B Molecular and Developmental Evolution 285: 146–57.

42. Longrich, N. R., and P. J. Currie. 2009. "A microraptorine (Dinosauria–Dromaeosauridae) from the Late Cretaceous of North America." *Proceedings of the National Academy of Sciences* 106 (13): 5002–7.

43. Chatterjee, S., and R. J. Templin. 2007. "Biplane wing planform and flight performance of the feathered dinosaur *Microraptor gui*." *Proceedings of the National Academy of Sciences* 104 (5): 1576–80.

44. Senter, P., R. Barsold, B. B. Britt, and D. A. Burnham. 2004. "Systematics and evolution of Dromaeosauridae (Dinosauria, Theropoda)." *Bulletin of the Gunma Museum of Natural History* 8: 1–20.

45. Xu, X., Z. Zhou, X. Wang, X. Kuang, F. Zhang, and X. Du. 2003. "Four-winged dinosaurs from China." *Nature* 421 (6921): 335–40.

46. Hone, D. W. E., H. Tischlinger, X. Xu, and F. Zhang. 2010. "The extent of the preserved feathers on the four-winged dinosaur *Microraptor gui* under ultraviolet light." *PLoS ONE* 5 (2): e9223.

47. Turner, Alan H., Diego Pol, Julia A. Clarke, Gregory M. Erickson, and Mark A. Norell. 2007. "A basal dromaeosaurid and size evolution preceding avian flight." *Science* 317: 1378–81.

48. Gianechini, F. A., P. J. Makovicky, and S. Apesteguía. 2011. "The teeth of the unenlagiine theropod *Buitreraptor* from the Cretaceous of Patagonia, Argentina, and the unusual dentition of the Gondwanan dromaeosaurids." *Acta Palaeontologica Polonica* 56 (2): 279–90.

49. Hu, D., L. Hou, L. Zhang, and X. Xu. 2009. "A pre-*Archaeopteryx* troodontid theropod from China with long feathers on the metatarsus." *Nature* 461 (7264): 640–43.

50. Coria, R. A., and L. Salgado. 1996. "A basal iguanodontian (Ornithischia: Ornithopoda) from the Late Cretaceous of South America." *Journal of Vertebrate Paleontology* 16: 445–57.

51. Salgado, L., R. A. Coria, and S. Heredia. 1997. "New materials of *Gasparinisaura cincosaltensis* (Ornithischia: Ornithopoda) from the Upper Cretaceous of Argentina." *Journal of Paleontology* 71: 933–40.

52. Cerda, Ignacio A. 2008. "Gastroliths in an ornithopod dinosaur." *Acta Palaeontologica Polonica* 53 (2): 351–55.

53. Norell, Mark A., and Peter J. Makovicky. 1999. "Important features of the dromaeosaurid skeleton II: information from newly collected specimens of *Velociraptor mongoliensis.*" *American Museum Novitatse* 3282: 1–45.

54. Maxwell, W. D., and L. M. Witmer. 1996. "New Material of *Deinonychus* (Dinosauria, Theropoda)." *Journal of Vertebrate Paleontology* 16 (3): 51A.

55. Witmer, Lawrence M., and William D. Maxwell. 1996. "The skull of *Deinonychus* (Dinosauria: Theropoda): New insights and implications." *Journal of Vertebrate Paleontology* 16 (3): 73A.

56. Chen, Z.-Q., and S. Lubin. 1997. "A fission track study of the terrigenous sedimentary sequences of the Morrison and Cloverly Formations in northeastern Bighorn Basin, Wyoming." *The Mountain Geologist* 34: 51–62.

57. Grellet-Tinner, G., and P. Makovicky. 2006. "A possible egg of the dromaeosaur *Deinonychus antirrhopus*: phylogenetic and biological implications." *Canadian Journal of Earth Sciences* 43: 705–19.

58. Erickson, Gregory M., Kristina Curry Rogers, David J. Varricchio, Mark A. Norell, and Xing Xu. 2007. "Growth patterns in brooding dinosaurs reveals the timing of sexual maturity in non-avian dinosaurs and genesis of the avian condition." *Biology Letters* 3 (5): 558–61.

59. Olshevsky, G. 2000. "An annotated checklist of dinosaur species by continent." *Mesozoic Meanderings* 3: 1–157.

60. Prum, R., and A. H. Brush. 2002. "The evolutionary origin and diversification of feathers." *The Quarterly Review of Biology* 77 (3): 261–95.

61. Turner, A. H., P. J. Makovicky, and M. A. Norell. 2007. "Feather quill knobs in the dinosaur *Velociraptor.*" *Science* 317 (5845): 1721.

62. Godefroit, Pascal, Philip J. Currie, Li Hong, Shang Chang Yong; and Dong Zhi-ming. 2008. "A new species of *Velociraptor* (Dinosauria: Dromaeosauridae) from the Upper Cretaceous of northern China." *Journal of Vertebrate Paleontology* 28 (2): 432–38.

63. Barsbold, Rinchen, and Halszka Osmólska. 1999. "The skull of *Velociraptor* (Theropoda) from the Late Cretaceous of Mongolia." *Acta Palaeontologica Polonica* 44 (2): 189–219.

64. Ostrom, John H. 1969. "Osteology of *Deinonychus antirrhopus*, an unusual theropod from the Lower Cretaceous of Montana." *Bulletin of the Peabody Museum of Natural History* 30: 1–165.

65. Swisher, Carl C., Yuan-qing Wang, Xiao-lin Wang, Xing Xu, and Yuan Wang. 1999. "Cretaceous age for the feathered dinosaurs of Liaoning, China." *Nature* 400: 58–61.

66. Xu, X., Z. Zhou, and R. O. Prum. 2001. "Branched integumental structures in *Sinornithosaurus* and the origin of feathers." *Nature* 410: 200–204.

67. Zhang, Fucheng, Stuart L. Kearns, Patrick J. Orr, Michael J. Benton, Zhonghe Zhou, Diane Johnson, Xing Xu, and Xiaolin Wang. 2010. "Fossilized melanosomes and the colour of Cretaceous dinosaurs and birds." *Nature* 463 (7284): 1075–78.

68. Lü, Junchang, Li Xu, Xingliao Zhang, Qiang Ji, Songhai Jia, Weiyong Hu, Jiming Zhang, and Yanhua Wu. 2007. "New dromaesoaurid dinosaur from the Late Cretaceous Qiupa Formation of Luanchuan area, western Henan, China." *Geological Bulletin of China* 26 (7): 777–86.

69. Zheng, Xiaoting, Xing Xu, Hailu You, Qi Zhao, and Zhiming Dong. 2010. "A short-armed dromaeosaurid from the Jehol Group of China with implications for early dromaeosaurid evolution." *Proceedings of the Royal Society B* 277 (1679): 211–17.

70. Bonde, N., and P. Christiansen. 2003. "New dinosaurs from Denmark." *Comptes Rendus Palevol* 2: 13–26.

71. Dong, Z.-M., and P. Currie. 1996. "On the discovery of an oviraptorid skeleton on a nest of eggs at Bayan Mandahu, Inner Mongolia, People's Republic of China." *Canadian Journal of Earth Sciences* 33: 631–36.

72. Clark, J. M., M. A. Norell, and R. Barsbold. 2001. "Two new oviraptorids (Theropoda: Oviraptorosauria), upper Cretaceous Djadokhta Formation, Ukhaa Tolgod, Mongolia." *Journal of Vertebrate Paleontology* 21 (2): 209–13.

73. Norell, M. A., J. M. Clark, L. M. Chiappe, and D. Dashzeveg. 1995. "A nesting dinosaur." *Nature* 378: 774–76.

74. Zhou, Z., and X. Wang. 2000. "A new species of *Caudipteryx* from the Yixian Formation of Liaoning, northeast China." *Vertebrata Palasiatica* 38 (2): 113–30.

75. Zhou, Z., X. Wang, F. Zhang, and X. Xu. 2000. "Important features of *Caudipteryx*: Evidence from two nearly complete new specimens." *Vertebrata Palasiatica* 38 (4): 241–54.

76. Jones, T. D., J. O. Farlow, J. A. Ruben, D. M. Henderson, and W. J. Hillenius. 2000. "Cursoriality in bipedal archosaurs." *Nature* 406 (6797): 716–18.

77. Xu, X., and M. A. Norell. 2006. "Non-Avian dinosaur fossils from the Lower Cretaceous Jehol Group of western Liaoning, China." *Geological Journal* 41: 419–37.

78. Dyke, G. J., and M. A. Norell. 2005. "*Caudipteryx* as a non-avialan theropod rather than a flightless bird." *Acta Palaeontologica Polonica* 50 (1): 101–16.

79. Xu, X., Q. Tan, J. Wang, X. Zhao, and L. Tan. 2007. "A gigantic bird-like dinosaur from the Late Cretaceous of China." *Nature* 447: 844–47.

80. Zhang, F., Z. Zhou, X. Xu, and X. Wang. 2002. "A juvenile coelurosaurian theropod from China indicates arboreal habits." *Naturwissenschaften* 89: 394–98.

81. Senter, P. 2007. "A new look at the phylogeny of Coelurosauria (Dinosauria: Theropoda)." *Journal of Systematic Palaeontology* 5 (4): 429–63.

82. Zhang, F., Z. Zhou, X. Xu, X. Wang, and C. Sullivan. 2008. "A bizarre Jurassic maniraptoran from China with elongate ribbon-like feathers." Nature 455 (7216): 1105–8.

83. Sekiya, T., and Z. Dong. 2010. "A New Juvenile Specimen of *Lufengosaurus huenei* Young 1941 (Dinosauria: Prosauropoda) from the Lower Jurassic Lower Lufeng Formation of Yunnan, Southwest China." *Acta Geologica Sinica* 84 (1): 11–21.

84. Young, C.-C. 1941. "A complete osteology of *Lufengosaurus huenei* Young (gen. et sp. nov.) from Lufeng, Yunnan, China." *Palaeontologia Sinica*, New Series C 7: 1–59.

85. Bonnan, M. F. 2003. "The evolution of manus shape in sauropod dinosaurs: implications for functional morphology, forelimb orientation, and phylogeny." *Journal of Vertebrate Paleontology* 23: 595–613.

86. Sander, P. M., O. Mateus, T. Laven, and N. Knötschke. 2006. "Bone histology indicates insular dwarfism in a new Late Jurassic sauropod dinosaur." *Nature* 441: 739–41.

87. Weishampel, D., D. B. Norman, and D. Grigorescu. 1993. "*Telmatosaurus transsylvanicus* from the Late Cretaceous of Romania: the most basal hadrosaurid dinosaur." *Palaeontology* 36: 361–85.

88. D'Emic, M. D., and B. Z. Foreman. 2012. "The beginning of the sauropod dinosaur hiatus in North America: insights from the Lower Cretaceous Cloverly Formation of Wyoming." *Journal of Vertebrate Paleontology* 32 (4): 883–902.

89. Young, C. C., and X.-J. Zhao. 1972. "*Mamenchisaurus hochuanensis* sp. nov." *Institute of Vertebrate Paleontology and Paleoanthropology Monographs* A 8: 1–30.

90. Hou, L.-H., S.-W. Zhou, and S.-C. Chao. 1976. "New discovery of sauropod dinosaurs from Sichuan." *Vertebrata PalAsiatica* 14 (3): 160–65.

91. Wedel, M. J., and R. L. Cifelli. 2005. "*Sauroposeidon*: Oklahoma's native giant." *Oklahoma Geology Notes* 65 (2): 40–57.

92. Dong, Z., S. Zhou, and Y. Zhang. 1983. "Dinosaurs from the Jurassic of Sichuan." *Palaeontologica Sinica*, New Series C 162 (23): 1–136.

93. Dong, Zhiming, G. Peng, and D. Huang. 1989. "The discovery of the bony tail club of sauropods." *Vertebrata Palasiatica* 27: 219–24.

94. Chatterjee, S., and Z. Zheng. 2002. "Cranial anatomy of *Shunosaurus*, a basal sauropod dinosaur from the Middle Jurassic of China." *Zoological Journal of the Linnean Society* 136 (1): 145–69.

95. Knoll, F., R. C. Ridgely, F. Ortega, J. L. Sanz, and L. M. Witmer. 2013. "Neurocranial Osteology and Neuroanatomy of a Late Cretaceous Titanosaurian Sauropod from Spain (*Ampelosaurus* sp.)," edited by Richard J. Butler. *PLoS ONE* 8: e54991.

96. You, H.-L., D.-Q. Li, L.-Q. Zhou, and Q. Ji. 2008. "*Daxiatitan binglingi*: a giant sauropod dinosaur from the Early Cretaceous of China." *Gansu Geology* 17 (4): 1–10.

97. You, H., D. Li, L. Zhou, and Q. Ji. 2006. "*Huanghetitan liujiaxiaensis*, a new sauropod dinosaur from the Lower Cretaceous Hekou Group of Lanzhou Basin, Gansu Province, China." *Geological Review* 52 (5): 668–74.

98. Mazzetta, Gerardo V., Per Christiansen, and Richard A. Fariña. 2004. "Giants and Bizarres: Body Size of Some Southern South American Cretaceous Dinosaurs." *Historical Biology* 65: 1–13.

ZHAO Chuang and YANG Yang

&

PNSO's Scientific Art Projects Plan: Stories on Earth (2010–2070)

ZHAO Chuang and YANG Yang are two professionals who work together to create scientific art. Mr. ZHAO Chuang, a scientific artist, and Ms. YANG Yang, an author of scientific children's books, started working together when they jointly founded PNSO, an organization devoted to the research and creation of scientific art in Beijing on June 1, 2010. A few months later, they launched Scientific Art Projects Plan: Stories on Earth (2010–2070). The plan uses scientific art to create a captivating, historically accurate narrative. These narratives are based on the latest scientific research, focusing on the complex relationships between species, natural environments, communities, and cultures. The narratives consider the perspectives of human civilizations while exploring Earth's past, present, and future. The PNSO founders plan to spend sixty years to do research and create unique and engaging scientific art and literature for people around the world. They hope to share scientific knowledge through publications, exhibitions, and courses. PNSO's overarching goal is to serve research institutions and the general public, especially young people.

PNSO has independently completed or participated in numerous creative and research projects. The organization's work has been shared with and loved by thousands of people around the world. PNSO collaborates with professional scientists and has been invited to many key laboratories around the world to create scientific works of art. Many works produced by PNSO staff members have been published in leading journals, including *Nature*, *Science*, and *Cell*. The organization has always been committed to supporting state-of-the-art scientific explorations. In addition, a large number of illustrations completed by PNSO staff members have been published and cited in hundreds of well-known media outlets, including the *New York Times*, the *Washington Post*, the *Guardian*, *Asahi Shimbun*, the *People's Daily*, BBC, CNN, Fox News, and CCTV. The works created by PNSO staff members have been used to help the public better understand the latest scientific discoveries and developments. In the public education sector, PNSO has held joint exhibitions with scientific organizations, including the American Museum of Natural History and the Chinese Academy of Sciences. PNSO has also completed international cooperation projects with the World Young Earth Scientist Congress and the Earth Science Matters Foundation, thus helping young people in different parts of the world understand and appreciate scientific art.

KEY PROJECTS

I. Darwin: An Art Project of Life Sciences
*The models are all life-sized and are based on fossils found around the world
1.1 Dinosaur fossils
1.2 Pterosaur fossils
1.3 Aquatic reptile fossils
1.4 Ancient mammals of the Cenozoic Era
1.5 Chengjiang biota: animals in the Early Cambrian from fossils discovered in Chengjiang, Yunnan, China
1.6 Jehol biota: animals in the Mesozoic Era from fossils discovered in Jehol, Western Liaoning, China
1.7 Early and extinct humans
1.8 Ancient animals that coexisted with early and extinct humans
1.9 Modern humans
1.10 Animals of the *Felidae* family
1.11 Animals of the *Canidae* family
1.12 Animals of the Proboscidea order

1.13 Animals of the *Ursidae* family

II. Galileo: An Art Project of Constellations
2.1 Classical Greek mythological characters that relate to the eighty-eight modern constellations
2.2 Classical Greek mythological characters that relate to ten constellation guardian deities

III. Starland Paradise: A Project Creating a Wonderful Science Literary World for Children
3.1 Science Literature for Children series: *Starland Paradise: Dingdong Bear and Twinkle Dino*
3.2 Education courses developed using Science Literature for Children series: *Starland Paradise: Dingdong Bear and Twinkle Dino*
IV. Haven: A Scientific Art Project about Our World
4.1 Guanguan: I Have a T-rex, A Science Literary Project for Children
4.2 Guanguan: I Have a Zoo, A Science Comic Project
4.3 The 12 Chinese Zodiac Animals, A Science Literary Project for Children

V. Laborer: Scientific Art Project to Express Humans' Production Activities
5.1 Common food crops
5.2 Common fruits
5.3 Common vegetables
5.4 Labor and Creation: Based on the Processes and Results of Humans' Production Activities

VI. Great Rivers: An Art Project on the History of Human Civilization
6.1 Great Thinkers in Human History from the Perspective of Scientific Art

6.2 Natural Landscape and Human Cultural Heritage: the Case of Mount Tai, China
6.3 Geographical Landscape and Life Phenomenon: the Case of Tanzania
6.4 Man-Made Landscape and Natural Environment: the Case of Beijing

Saichania

Microraptor

Pachycephalosaurus

Olorotitan

Triceratops

Stygimoloch

Mononykus

Nodosaurus

Sinosauropteryx

Tatisaurus

Tyrannosaurus

Protoceratops

Stygimoloch

Stegoceras

Triceratops

Dromaeosaurus

Tatisaurus

Stegoceras

Sinosauropteryx

Tyrannosaurus

Mononykus

Achelousaurus

Stegosaurus

Mamenchisaurus

Centrosaurus

Dromaeosaurus

Pachycephalosaurus

Achelousaurus

Microraptor

Huayangosaurus

Therizinosaurus

Rajasaurus

Wuerhosaurus

Triceratops

Centrosaurus

Spinosaurus

Wuerhosaurus